D. A. De MATTEO

R. F. MUNROE

FALL 1984

COACHING THE DEFENSIVE SECONDARY

COACHING
THE
DEFENSIVE
SECONDARY

Mark Aubrey Schuster

Parker Publishing Company, Inc. West Nyack, New York

© 1984 *by*

Parker Publishing Company, Inc.

West Nyack, New York

Library of Congress Cataloging in Publication Data

Schuster, Mark A.
　　Coaching the defensive secondary.

　　Includes index.
　　1. Football—Defense.　2. Football coaching.
I. Title.
GV951.18.S38　1984　　　796.332′2　　　84-7770
ISBN 0-13-138942-4

Printed in the United States of America

Dedication

There are many persons in almost everyone's life who help him accomplish any task. I would like to dedicate this book to those who have helped me to become what I am today—

My father, Richard Mark Schuster

My mother, Lu Jean Schuster

My grandfather, Charles Aubrey Gibson

My grandmother, Mildred May Gibson, who has been a special inspiration to me through some very difficult times.

A special dedication to Karen Schlothayeur, who helped me to continue when "quitting" would have been so easy.

And, to my wife, Debbie, and our children (mine by marriage), Craig, Kristen and Tracy, for their support and understanding and the time they gave me to work on this book.

Acknowledgments

This book was written in a period of two months. It is concerned with the knowledge I have endeavored to impart through my teaching for the past twelve years.

No coach begins his career being all-knowledgeable about the sport he coaches or knowing the best methods to employ in teaching the techniques he feels are necessary to make his players successful. We are always learning by reading, listening and observing at clinics and talking with other coaches.

In this book I have written about what I learned as a player and the knowledge I have gleaned through my experiences as a coach as to what is necessary to make good defensive backs better.

It is very conceivable that many, or at least some, of the phrases used and ideas proposed in this book have been uttered before by football mentors. Therefore, if something sounds familiar to others, so be it. Memories of advice given and knowledge gained in the past tend to become one's own.

I would like to thank all coaches for this book. If it weren't for their willingness to share ideas with others, football would not be the great game it is today. My thanks for their sharing with me.

A special note of gratitude is owed Coach John Strycula of Citrus Junior College, Azusa, California, for his time and patience. It is from him, especially, that I learned so much of what is written in this book.

INTRODUCTION

Defensive football has become more and more complex in the last few years. Since the wide-spread use of devastating offensive styles, such as the veer option, wishbone and control passing attacks, coaches have found it necessary to commit their secondary personnel quickly into run support as well as short zone coverage. The key to controlling the strong complex offensive attack is not just a good secondary coverage, but multiple secondary coverages. Many teams in the past relied on either a strong zone coverage or a good man coverage for their entire season. With improved scouting techniques and offenses geared to beat the secondary with crossing patterns, delays, picks, counter options, boot-legs, motion and play-action passes, successful coaches today must enter a ball game with the ability to adjust their coverages.

The most important feature of pass defense today is to have the ability to adjust to the many variations in formations and situations presented by today's offenses.

In today's game of football just one or two secondary covers will not do. Most pass offenses today, in order to be successful, must control or at least influence the safeties. The responsibility of the secondary as a whole and the safeties themselves has never been more critical to a defense's chances for success. A pass offense must be able to determine the safeties' assigned duties in order to successfully attack the defense.

The secondary is not only required to handle specific pass assignments, but the increased emphasis on attacking the corner with the running game, has placed an overload on the defensive complexities involved in the run support for the perimeter.

To control offenses which run veer options, wishbone and power attacks and still play sound pass defense against play-action, flare control, and delay-passing attacks, a defense must have a flexible secondary that covers all possible situations without confusion.

9

It is important for the whole defense to understand that good secondary coverage and run support require five things of the defensive team as a unit:

1. Line rush.
2. Defensive secondary always in the same cover and proper position.
3. Ability to change your cover to be in the best defensive situation versus any offensive formations.
4. Ability to force receivers out of their intended routes.
5. Ability to identify runs quickly and lend proper support.

At Citrus College, Azusa, California, we run man, zone and combinations of both. We have nine different covers with a few variations off three of them. All of our covers build from a basic zone or man defense.

We try to disguise our safeties in some defenses but see no need in many of them. This book will describe all nine covers and variations, including reads, keys and coaching points.

Mark Aubrey Schuster

CONTENTS

COACHING THE DEFENSIVE SECONDARY

1

PASS OFFENSES AND PASSING TRENDS

In order to understand pass defense it is imperative for a secondary coach to be a student of pass offense. To successfully defend the pass the coach must understand what pass offenses are trying to do to his defense. He must also understand the weaknesses of each secondary cover and know when each cover is a poor gamble.

Delay Pass Attack

The theory of this attack is to allow the defense to react to what appears to be a deep pass route. The primary receiver will disguise his intentions until the last second. He can disguise what he is going to do by faking a block, faking a slow drag in the wrong direction or just standing or delaying for a count.

The delaying action gets the defense to momentarily commit itself to deeper receivers. The delaying receiver then exploits their neglect of the shallow zones by breaking into a short underzone left open by the retreating defense. Most delays are run from one of two primary formations. However, they can be run from any set. The most favorite formation is the *slot*. From this formation the offense can run the defense off with either the X or Z and use the other receiver on the underneath delay pattern. (The letters X, Y and Z are a coaching shorthand. X refers to the split end, Y refers to the tight end, while Z refers to the flanker.)

The other formation is the *pro set*. When the pro set is used, most teams will delay the tight end or a running back. The wide receivers are too obvious to delay in this set. Many delays come off play-action fakes.

There are two basic ways to beat a team with the delay. The first and most obvious is to let the linebackers drop off and then throw the ball to the delay receiver in front of them. Diagrams 1:1 through 1:5 and 1:7 and 1:8 are of this type. The second delay comes from play action with a fake block to draw the linebackers up after which the receiver tries to work his way into the outside zone or the area just behind the linebackers. Diagrams 1:6 and 1:9 are of this type.

Delays from the Pro Sets—Diagrams 1:1 to 1:9

Diagram 1:1. Tight end delay with linebackers going to the curl

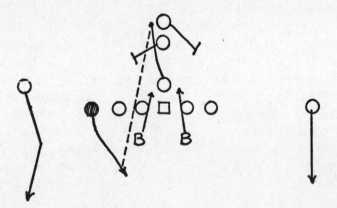

Diagram 1:2. Some teams will automatic to T.E. delays to avoid blitzes.

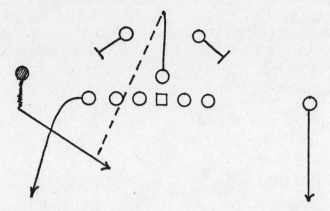

Diagram 1:3. Flankers will delay under T.E. patterns. They will work to catch the ball in front of LB.

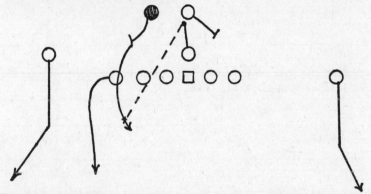

Diagram 1:4. Backs will delay out in front of LB from either side. Some teams will send backs when they read an outside blitz.

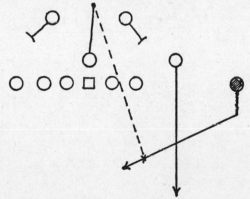

Diagram 1:5. Delays from the slot set. X moves off the line, slowly waits until the LB clears the area.

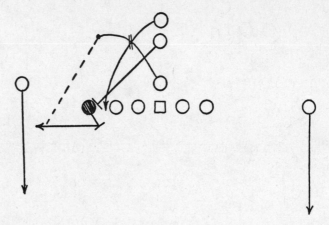

Diagram 1:6. T.E. plays fake delay to the outside, then breaks to the open area in front of the flat cover.

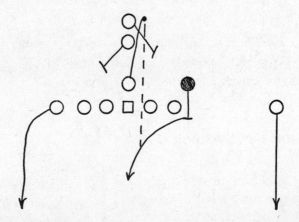

Diagram 1:7. Tight slot fakes block and then breaks in front of linebackers.

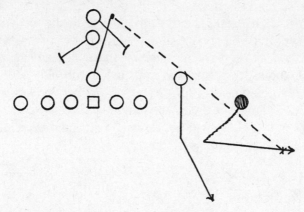

Diagram 1:8. X starts delay pattern to the inside and then breaks back to the outside.

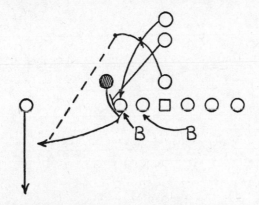

Diagram 1:9. Tight slot fakes block with play-action fake and then breaks to the outside after drawing linebacker up.

Play-Action Pass Attack

The play-action passing attack is an integral part of any team's offense that can run the ball effectively. It serves as a natural complement to any good running game. The play-action pass is many times used by teams as a surprise weapon in short-yardage or goal-line situations. The play action is an effective weapon against a stunting defense.

Action passes are most effective on first downs to keep the defense off balance. Most teams prefer to run them more against zones rather than man-for-man defenses. Play-action passes can force rotating secondary covers to rotate into a predicted direction and take advantage of the zone's weak spots. It appears that most teams run play-action passes from an "I" formation. This allows quick linebacker and secondary reads which will influence their zone rotations. Favorite patterns of the play-action teams are *drags*, *curls*, *slants*, *looks* and *streaks*. Diagrams 1:10-1:15 show common play-action passes:

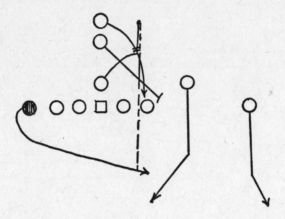

Diagram 1:10. Very popular is Y under on a drag from the "I" slot.

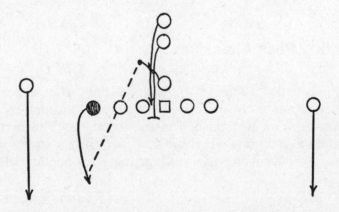

Diagram 1:11. Y look from power play.

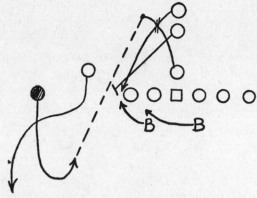

Diagram 1:12. Outside power fake X curl. Draws LB up to catch the ball behind him.

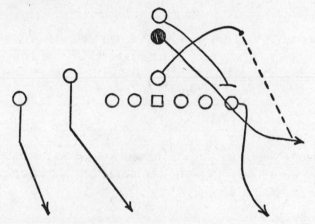

Diagram 1:13. Weak side flood from slot. Back runs at the end as if to block then slips into the flat.

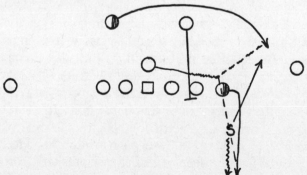

Diagram 1:14. Veer Pop Pass. QB looks at strong safety. If strong safety comes for Pitch, QB throws to the T.E.; if the strong safety retreats with the T.E., QB will pitch the ball to the trailing back.

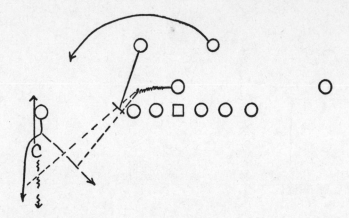

Diagram 1:15. Weak side Veer Pop Pass. QB looks at the corner. If the corner comes up, the receiver runs a fade; the QB then throws the ball over the corner and in front of the safety. If the corner retreats, the receiver runs a slant—the QB must hit him quickly.

Play action has many possible patterns—too many to put them all down. However, such things as play actions, screens, reverse passes and double passes must be considered by the secondary coach.

The Bootleg Passes

The bootleg is a play-action pass; however, it goes against the flow and can foul up most secondary reads so badly it is important to discuss it as a different offensive weapon. The bootleg attempts to get the defense to commit to a point of attack away from where the play is really going to attack. It can turn into either a run or a pass. If run with good execution, the bootleg can be an offense in itself. Most bootlegs today like to run Y across or Z across, although some still run the curl and out patterns. The bootleg is slow enough to allow good receivers to appear to be challenging the deep zones and then break off their patterns at 18 to 20 yards. Common bootleg patterns are shown in Diagrams 1:16-1:21:

It is possible to run very effective screens from a bootleg attack as well as from the patterns shown here.

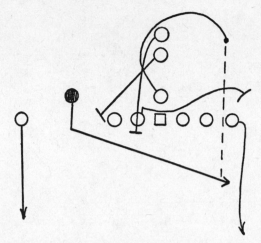

Diagram 1:16. Bootleg Z across. Pattern is run at 15 yards.

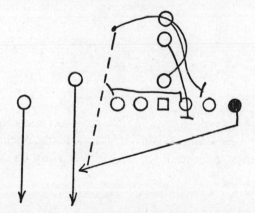

Diagram 1:17. Bootleg Y across. This pattern is run at 15 yards.

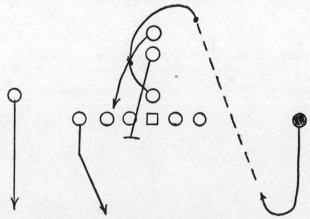

Diagram 1:18. Bootleg X 20-yard curl.

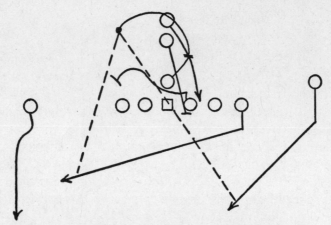

Diagram 1:19. Bootleg Y across or Z throw back.

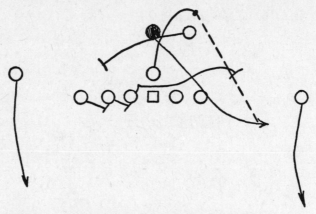

Diagram 1:20. Back through the line and into the flat.

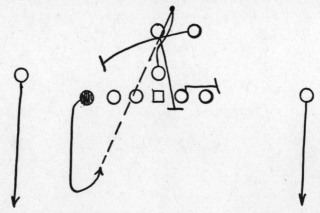

Diagram 1:21. T.E. throw back at 20 yards.

The Control-Pass Attack

The Control-Pass Attack is just what it says—a short, high percentage attack. In this attack many offenses use motion to change formation strength to achieve the advantage of an overload at the snap of the ball. With this motion they can put three quick receivers to one side or two quick receivers to each side at the same time. Whether a team motions a third receiver to one side or comes out in a formation with three receivers set to one side, we refer to this situation as *"Trips."* If a team uses motion to put two receivers on each side of their formation or they come to the line of scrimmage with two receivers on each side, we refer to this situation as *"Twins."*

Diagrams 1:22 to 1:29 show methods by which the offense can get into twin and trip sets:

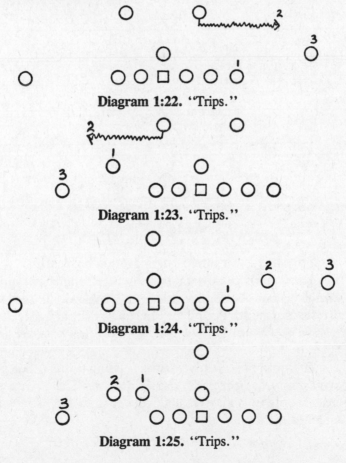

Diagram 1:22. "Trips."

Diagram 1:23. "Trips."

Diagram 1:24. "Trips."

Diagram 1:25. "Trips."

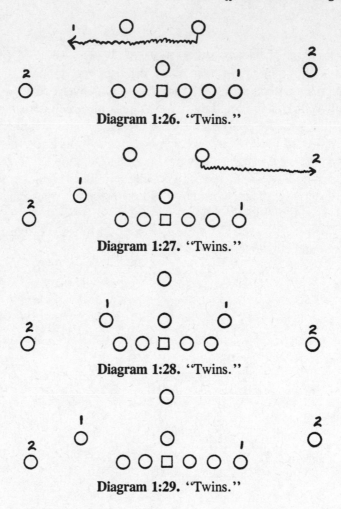

Diagram 1:26. "Twins."

Diagram 1:27. "Twins."

Diagram 1:28. "Twins."

Diagram 1:29. "Twins."

Trips and Twins are used to overload zones.

The control attack uses many receivers in short, quick or under patterns to control offensive drives with five to eight yard strikes. This attack uses slants, drags, hitches and quick-outs to free receivers. Backs are used to control LB positioning. Common patterns are shown in Diagrams 1:30-1:35. There are many more possible combinations.

The objective of this attack is to create small holes in the pass coverage and hit them quick with short passes. The offense would like to force the defense into a five under cover so they could counter with the bomb against the two deep.

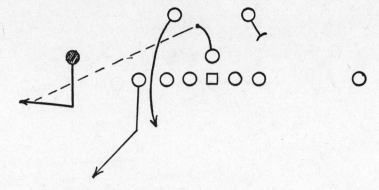

Diagram 1:30. Quick out, back is used to hold **LB**.

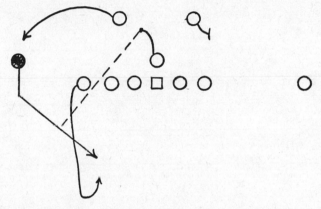

Diagram 1:31. Slant, back is used to pull safety out of pattern.

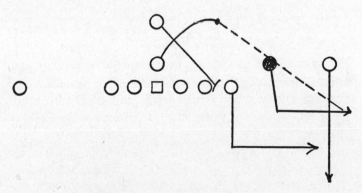

Diagram 1:32. Flood from trips.

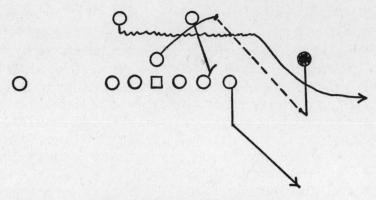

Diagram 1:33. Hitch from trips.

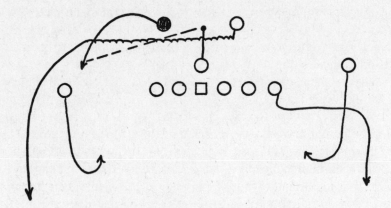

Diagram 1:34. Swingback from twins.

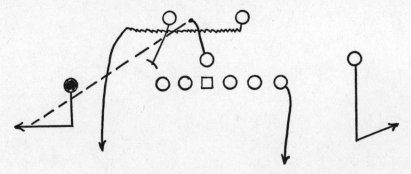

Diagram 1:35. Quick out from twins.

Dropback Pass Offense

The dropback pass is probably the simplest form of the passing attack; however, it forces the defense to cover all zones from sideline to sideline. This forces the defense to cover both deep and short zones and does not give up the intended play side until just before release. It makes it almost impossible for the defense to squeeze down the zones or overload an area. The dropback attack can use many types of screen patterns: The middle screen to backs, slot or tight end, outside quick screens to wide receivers, outside screens to backs, and double screens to both sides. Most dropback passes will use their backs in flare control to hold linebackers in position or to move them out of a reception area. Backs are also primary receivers in the dropback attack and are used to combat blitzes by breaking into the areas where the linebacker left to catch a quick pass. Diagrams 1:36 to 1:41 show the use of backs to hold the defense in controlled areas. This allows other receivers to break into uncovered areas.

The dropback passing game has many keys and reads. It is important for the secondary to understand what the quarterback is reading or keying. The reads allow the quarterback and receiver to get the best pass route and cut in the weakest area of the defense due to their cover. The quarterback read, if it is right, increases the chances for a completion, cuts down on interceptions and gives the offense its best chances for success. It is important for the defensive backs to disguise their covers as long as possible. This may cause a late read by the quarterback. The better the quarterback is at reading your defense, the more often you

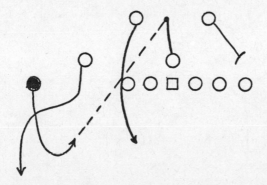

Diagram 1:36. X curl with the halfback running inside to hold LB.

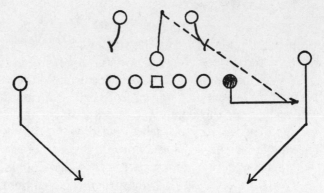

Diagram 1:37. Y out with maximum protection, both backs stay in.

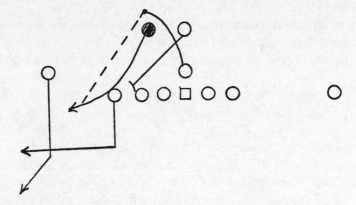

Diagram 1:38. Strong flood tight end holds strong safety off if defense is in a zone.

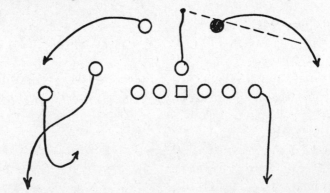

Diagram 1:39. Both backs swing for quick outside patterns.

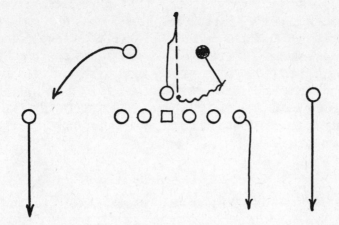

Diagram 1:40. Fullback middle screen with halfback drawing weak backer off.

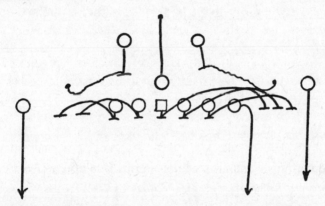

Diagram 1:41. Double screen QB can throw to either side.

must change your covers. It is important to be able to stop the same type of play with more than one defensive cover. This way, if the offense is beating your cover with a read or key, you have other ways to stop the play. We like to have three different covers to stop most outside patterns.

One of the hardest passes to defend comes from the dropback attack. It's called the timed or spot pass. In this type of attack the quarterback takes a predetermined number of steps to set up. This number is usually an odd number: three for quick passes; five steps for a

10- to 12-yard pass; seven steps for an 18-yard pass and bombs. The quarterback will take his last step and throw the ball to a receiver who has not yet turned to look for the ball. The ball is thrown one yard outside the receiver's shoulder to the side he is to turn. The receiver usually runs one more step before turning on three- and five-step patterns and two steps more before he turns on seven-step patterns. In this way the ball is almost to the receiver when he turns. This takes away the defensive back's ability to react to the ball once the receiver looks. This type of attack also takes a lot of practice time.

The Sprint Out Attack

The sprint out is an attack which can be either a run or pass. If the quarterback can clear the corner quickly and the linebackers are taking pass drops, he will run with the ball. If the corner is jammed up and/or the linebackers are playing for the run, the quarterback will throw the ball.

The big disadvantage of the sprint out has always been that it takes the defense to the side the ball is going to be thrown to and allows the defense to close down the zones. The only throw-backs have to be back side posts which are closing the zone into the safety area.

The sprint out was not designed to throw deep. It is a 10- to 15-yard offense.

The sprint out requires the quarterback to sprint five steps on a 45-degree angle from the center to a depth of not more than five yards behind the tackle to the right or left side. At this point he must challenge the line of scrimmage and determine whether to pass or run.

Azusa High School in California brought about an interesting change when they introduced a *Sprint Roll* into their sprint out offense. In the Sprint Roll series the quarterback sprints five steps to the right or left and at the point where he would challenge the line of scrimmage, he rolls back to the opposite side of his sprint. In the blocking scheme, the linemen drop their feet back to the side of the sprint to allow the defensive linemen to penetrate to the side the quarterback is sprinting. When the quarterback rolls back to the opposite side, the linemen lock out the defense or cut them. The defense is caught overplaying to the sprint side with the offense prepared to take advantage. In a well-drilled offense the receivers will change their patterns on their seventh step. Diagrams 1:42 through 1:45 show the sprint roll pass.

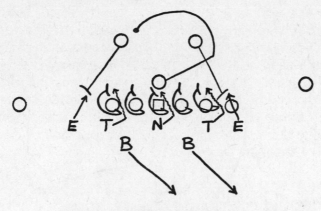

Diagram 1:42. Sprint roll blocking.

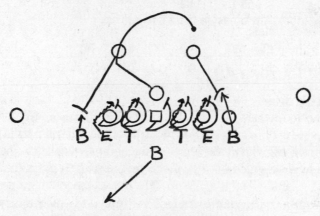

Diagram 1:43. Sprint roll blocking.

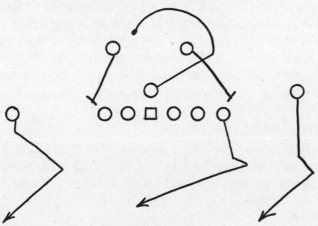

Diagram 1:44

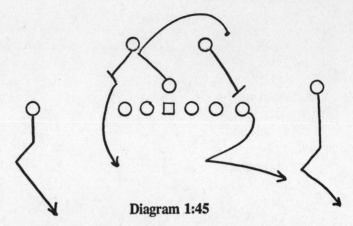

Diagram 1:45

Diagrams 1:44 and 1:45. Patterns run from the sprint roll series. Left half will hold, then release if no one comes.

Roll Out Passing Attack

The roll out pass is designed to take away the most effective part of pass defense, the pass *rush*! The objective of the roll out pass is to move the pass protection out of the center of the defensive attack to the outside where there is less pressure. By avoiding the rush, it gives the quarterback more time to pick his receiver. This makes the job of the secondary twice as hard. The longer the defense is forced to cover receivers, the better chance the receivers have of breaking free.

Fran Tarkington of the Minnesota Vikings showed the football world how the roll out makes it possible to avoid a rush and find receivers. The roll out is an outstanding attack to use delayed receivers, because the quarterback is slower in showing his intent to throw deep. This allows the defense to get deep drops, leaving the short zones open.

Trends in Pass Offense

Since the forward pass became legal on January 12, 1906, coaches have continually been finding ways to free receivers down field to strike quickly and cut deeply into the defense.

Notre Dame, with an end named Knute Rockne, awakened the football world to the forward pass in 1913 against Army at West Point.

Slowly at first, but with ever-gaining speed, the forward pass opened up the American game of football. The latest trends include controlled short passes, delayed backs and receivers, bootleg and running receivers under linebacker covers to the inside.

The concept selected by a particular coach will depend almost entirely upon the player material available.

The new concepts cause the defense to always be prepared for everything and anything. Pass theory can be broken down into four categories:

1. As a complement to aid the running game.
2. To supplement the running game when ball control is the game plan.
3. The pass offense—pass first, run second.
4. Third and long only—few coaches attempt the third and long only theory anymore. It gives the defense a tremendous advantage to know when you're going to pass.

Offenses at this time seem to like the first down, four- to five-yard pass. A quick-out, play-action slant, four-yard hitch, outside quick-screen or a tight-end quick pass off play action sets up a second and three or four which is what the offense would prefer to work with. Another favorite of delay pass can be thrown to backs setting up to block in the backfield for two counts and then slipping beyond the line of scrimmage to catch the ball in the area in front of the linebackers. This also can be thrown to a receiver who delays a count and runs under a deeper pattern being run by another receiver. This enables him to catch the ball in front of the linebackers. If a delayed back or receiver can split a seam after making the catch, you have a big gain or even a score.

The second and short down has become surprise time. Many teams will go for it all with a play fake into the line and a bomb being thrown to an outside receiver faking a block and running deep.

Third and five or less is spot-pass time. Most teams, if they are going to throw on this down, will throw at a spot 12 to 15 yards to the sideline, curl, short pass or corner. This spot pass is many times referred to as possession pass. Today on third and short the bootleg pass is popular. On a bootleg, the quarterback will fake a power-type play into the line to one side, pull a guard and roll back to the other side to throw. If the secondary is reading flow, this causes them to roll away from the intended receiver and will leave the corner back with a one-on-one situation, even if the team is in a zone. Bootleg patterns used to be only bombs; now, however, many coaches use them for the 18-yard out or 18-yard curl.

The third and long has become (due in part, I believe, to the Dallas shotgun formation) the down for the widespread formations with four or five wide receivers, motion, reverse passes, or fake draw and screen. On third and long the secondary must be prepared for almost anything. Some teams today even throw a regular sideline, curl, post, or corner pattern.

The coach must have in his defensive arsenal not only one way but at least two ways to combat each type of attack.

2

THE RUNNING ATTACK

Running Attacks

Never before has it been so important for the secondary to read for and react to the run. Many teams today run ball control defenses, which is to say, "Three yards and a cloud of dust." They pound away at defenses and wait for them to make a mistake. Once the offense finds the defense adjusting to the inside, the attack swings swiftly to the corner and they arc off and running. This style of offense is typified by the triple option. The term, triple option, can mean many things to a secondary. The formation from which it is run is the biggest factor in deciding what cover the secondary should be in. If the opponent runs an option offense, it is most important for the secondary coach to know which type: the Wishbone, Houston, Power I, I Slot or the Cincinnati style of option football.

What does each type of option try to do? Regardless of the type of option, formation or mechanics used to implement it, the basics of the triple option are about the same. The offense wants to isolate both the defensive tackle and defensive end and force them to commit themselves, while at the same time, they want to force the secondary to play pass as long as receivers are running down the field. The offense has two backs who can lead the play or fake into the line to hold the linebackers inside. Run support from the secondary comes in two forms: primary and secondary. Who will be the primary defensive back depends on the cover and situation; however, the primary back, no matter which back it is, has two immediate requirements. He cannot allow the ball carrier a clean, straight path to the outside and he must close the running lane down and force the back to turn up inside. If he must attack a blocker, he must control the blocker's outside shoulder, so he appears to the outside. This will force the back to turn up inside to the pursuit.

The wide receivers and tight end can be very successful in delaying quick support from the secondary by using the stalk block. The stalk block is begun with a swift release from the line of scrimmage to back the defensive backs off. After a six-yard release, the receivers break down and start to stalk the defensive backs. The receivers let the defensive backs commit to the run and then block them whichever way they want to go, inside or out. It is most important for the defensive back to be schooled to attack quickly through the stalk block. He can never play around a stalk block. To play around it is to flirt with disaster. The defensive backs involved in primary run support must be schooled to attack the stalk blocker, while at the same time, the secondary run support must be taught to watch for a fake stalk block and then a release into a pass pattern.

The Houston veer attack is the toughest on defensive secondaries because it has two wide receivers besides the possible triple option attack. It can also be run from a split slot set. The split backs can run triple option or pro offense, plus the two wide receivers allow for a balanced passing attack as well.

The option offenses force the defense to commit the secondary in an effort to stop the run. If the secondary has to come up often enough to stop the run, chances are it will stop reading well and will just start playing run. This will cost them when the offense turns to play action and throws deep.

The option offense also allows for blockers coming down on the defensive backs on almost every play. From a wishbone or any three-backs offense the lead back is a blocker looking for a corner back. The end will release up field, looking to block the safety (Diagrams 2:1 and 2:2).

This means that once the secondary reads run and can come to help, they must fight off blockers before they can lend support to stop the run.

In the veer offense as in an "I" offense or a slot offense, the blockers are the receivers. The receivers can either cross block the play or straight block it (Diagrams 2:3 and 2:4).

The advantage of the straight block is that the receivers can cut with backs straight over them, whereas the cross block, with the receiver

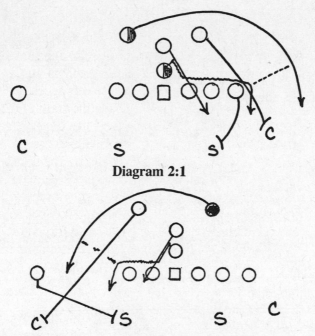

Diagram 2:1

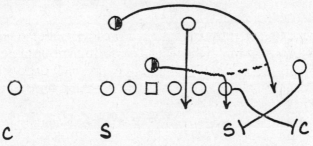

Diagram 2:2. Backs can cut defensive backs—wide receivers can't, unless they come straight at the defensive back.

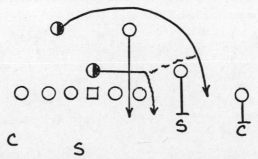

Diagram 2:3. Blocking of the Houston veer offense.

Diagram 2:4. Straight block from the split slot veer.

coming down to the inside from the blind side, must block above the waist.

This increased emphasis on the outside running game has put more pressure on the secondary to help with perimeter run support.

Sweep. The sweep is another form of the strong outside attack which the secondary must lead with swift and decisive run support. The sweep must be recognized quickly so that the defensive back can get to the line of scrimmage to take on the lead blockers in a good hitting position.

Counters. Counter options can have devastating effects on secondaries which react too quickly to the offense's first steps. Counter options are run and blocked the same as a regular option. The only difference is that they start in the opposite direction from where they are really going. The idea is to get the secondary to commit itself to the wrong side (Diagrams 2:5 and 2:6).

The counter option in the wishbone can mis-key the secondary and cost them important steps in the wrong direction, resulting in lost time and yards gained (Diagrams 2:7 and 2:8).

The secondary must always be alert to the possibility of the option reverse, a counter play which can hit quickly inside. Inside counters are usually not covered by primary run support. However, any and all runs must be contained by the secondary run support. The secondary run support backs must always contain any breakaways and try to pinch them off between the middle safety and the outside cover whether it is a safety or corner back. Diagrams 2:9 and 2:10 show the breakaway being pinched off first towards the primary support and then with a cutback against the primary support.

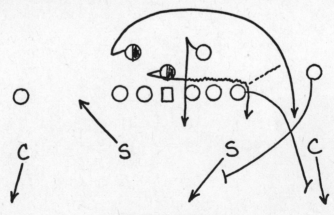

Diagram 2:5

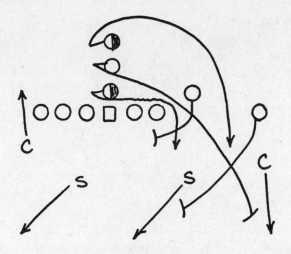

Diagram 2:6

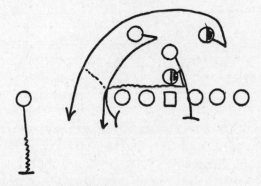

Diagram 2:7. Counter Option from the Wishbone to the split side.

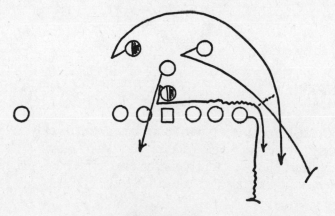

Diagram 2:8

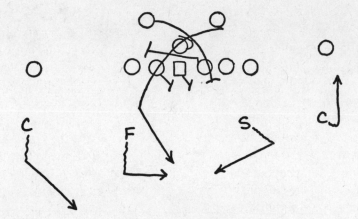

Diagram 2:9. The safety must keep an inside-out angle on the ball and the outside contain must keep an outside-in angle on the ball.

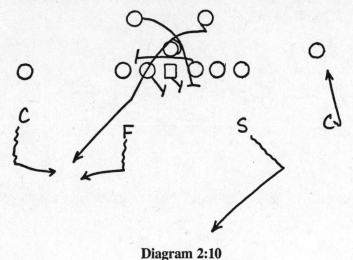

Diagram 2:10

Quick Pitch

The quick pitch is the type of play that, if read quickly and reacted to properly, should not give a good secondary any problems. The only way it can beat you is if your corners don't read. The quick pitch is more of an element of surprise than a total offense.

The quick pitch must be stopped at or behind the line of scrimmage. If it isn't stopped there and the play is allowed to turn upfield, you can be in big trouble. The key to the quick pitch is to get the guard and tackle on the play side to get out in front quickly and knock down the cornerback, if he's slow in coming up. The fullback will drive into the line for a possible trap play. His primary job is to hold the linebackers and cut any linemen in pursuit. In most quick pitch offenses a good counter is to fake the pitch to the weak side and hit the tight end with a quick pass. These two counters, the fullback trap inside and the quick pass to the tight end, are designed to hold the linebackers inside and put the pressure for the quick pitch on the secondary. If at any time the linebackers are getting outside to stop the pitch when it turns up, look for the offense to counter with the trap or the pass. Diagrams 2:11 through 2:14 show quick pitch counters.

There are many running attacks that the secondary must help contain. The off-tackle play is one of the toughest. The off-tackle can be

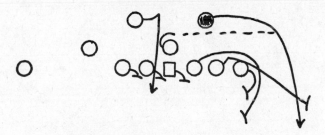

Diagram 2:11. Quick pitch from slot.

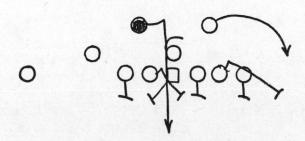

Diagram 2:12. Fake pitch fullback trap.

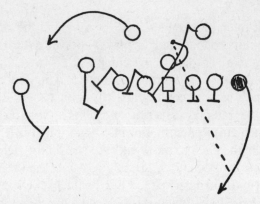

Diagram 2:13. Quick pass to tight end off pitch fake. The other counter from this play involves a fake pitch, a fake trap with a quick screen to the pitch man.

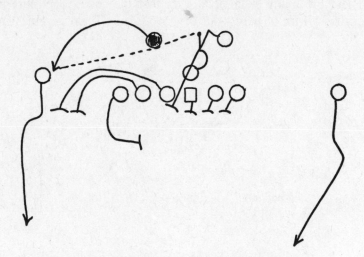

Diagram 2:14. Fake pitch, fake trap, quick screen.

attacked with an isolated block (Diagram 2:15), a power block (Diagram 2:16), veer block (Diagram 2:17), cross block (Diagram 2:18), hook block (Diagram 2:19) or a combination block (Diagram 2:20). The strong safety to the strong side and the free safety or weak corner to the weak side (on a double tight end offense) must be able to read this play and help inside or out. He must make his read, step up to within one yard of the defensive end and read the back's move inside or out. (Diagrams 2:21 and 2:22)

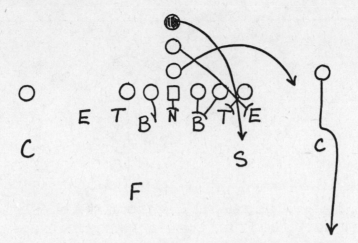

Diagram 2:15. Off-tackle can be attacked with an isolated block.

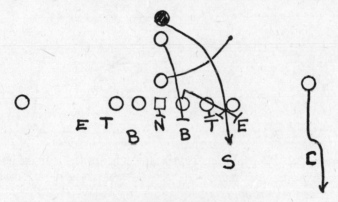

Diagram 2:16. Power block attack.

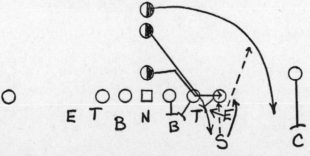

Diagram 2:17. In the veer block if the end takes the dive back the safety is left with the QB and pitch man. If the end takes the pitch, then the safety must read for the dive or QB to turn upfield.

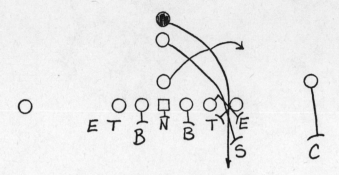

Diagram 2:18. Cross block attack.

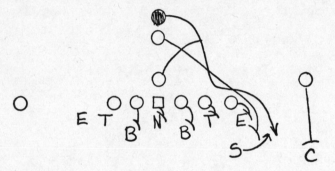

Diagram 2:19. The fullback will try to seal the corner, with the hook block on the end. When the safety reads hook block, he must come up quickly to the outside.

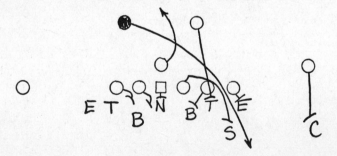

Diagram 2:20. The two things that must be done to stop this play no matter how it's blocked are: the strong end must close to the inside, and the strong safety must step up and read the back.

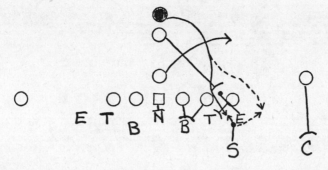

Diagram 2:21. The corner back to the tight end side when the offense is in a slot set must be able to make this same read and play. (**Diagram 2:22**)

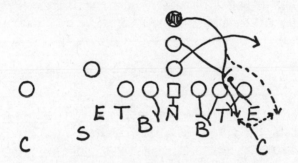

Diagram 2:22

With the complex offensive blocking patterns and different offensive attacks on the corners, the secondaries must be hard-hitting, skilled people who read well. Defensive football demands excellence from its secondary for both run and pass coverage.

Some of these techniques are obviously designed for an athlete with more talent than your average high school player. It is, in my opinion, most important to start basic reads on lower division teams. This helps to identify the player who can make the reads and give the athlete some knowledge of playing requirements for the varsity.

3

TECHNIQUES OF THE SECONDARY

In this section we are not going to tell you how to improve any of these areas. We will do that in Chapter 12 on drills. This chapter deals with what abilities and techniques a good defensive back must have.

Feet

Feet are probably one of the most important things a defensive back possesses. It is not enough that he be fast on his feet. He must be made to understand that there is no other position on the field that demands more from the feet than that of a defensive back. It is important to care for the feet and report any small problem that might develop into a major problem. A defensive back, playing on injured or irritated feet, will be less than effective when he has to bear down to reach the football. It is said that football is a game of inches; the secondary is a game of high-speed *steps*! One step in a key situation, one way or another, can make the difference.

Hips

The ability to have fluid hips enabling the defensive back to move from side to side without losing time in execution must be developed. The ability to change direction and lose no time in the process is what makes an All-American as opposed to just a defensive back. The ability to roll from the right side of a zone to the left side of one with the quarterback's eyes is a most important ability. To be able to meet a receiver coming at you, roll your hips and run with him is what effective defensive backs must be able to do.

Retreat

A defensive retreat should be low, bent at the waist, with the shoulder over the hips. This must be as normal as running forward. The defensive back must be smooth and rhythmic, reaching to the rear with his feet as he goes. It is important to keep the weight forward at all times. If a receiver breaks in front of the defensive back, he does not have to shift his weight forward in order to drive on the receiver's move. If he retreats with his weight back on his heels and a receiver breaks in front of him, he would have to plant his back foot and shift all his weight forward in order to drive on that move.

Lateral Movement

This is a must for a defensive back. Most interceptions come down to the ability of the defensive back to move laterally. Lateral movement is the key to a good closing zone defense. It is a primary ingredient in a good-pursuing defense. If a defensive back can't move laterally, he can't play in the secondary. We feel that a team's lateral movement is directly proportional to its defensive success.

Quickness

Quickness is the speed at which a defensive back can change direction and reach top speed in that new direction. A defensive back does not have to possess great foot speed if he has great quickness. This quickness can give him a jump on receivers and the football when it's in the air. Quickness is an absolute in a good tackler. It's important in tackling because a defensive back many times must lower his center of gravity and wait on a back in the open field to make the tackle. The quickness is necessary when the back suddenly changes direction. The quick defensive back will be able to adjust and make the tackle.

Forward Movement

Most defensive backs are taught to go backward and side-to-side; however, few are ever taught to come forward. Quickness coming forward is most desirable but few athletes are taught the primary technique. It is simple. The defensive back must take a short, quick-break step to stop his backward movement and to push off on that foot heading forward. It must be a *short step*. A long step gives him no forward power, takes too long, and there is the possibility that he will go down (slip and fall).

Reads

Defensive backs must have certain reads drilled into them every day. If a defensive back blows a read in a ball game, it can only be due to one of two things: the coach didn't work on the reads enough or the coach is playing an athlete who can't read. *Reads are the backbone of a secondary*. Well-selected reads can identify offensive intentions quickly enough for the defense to stop the plays before they get started.

A read is a simple clue to what the offense intends to do. An example would be: if the strong safety reads the offensive tight end blocking the defensive end out, we would look for the ball to go inside. A read can be as simple as the flow of the offensive backs or as complex as reading the tight end's many moves. It can be anything the coach feels will give his defensive backs a solid start in the right direction to stop the intended attack.

Keys

Keys are important to teach. A key can be as simple as the formation a team runs or how deep a back lines up. But, they must be taught. Keys help in alignment and defensive direction.

Keys usually come from scouting reports. If a certain team always runs from a pro set and always passes from a slot set, you have a good key as to what defense you may want to change to when your opponent comes out in a slot.

Hands

It is most important that a defensive back be taught to play a receiver's hands. This is important if a defensive back is beaten by two yards or more. He must be taught not to look for the ball. A perfect pass is a touchdown. As a receiver looks back to the quarterback, it automatically causes him to cross his hips which will slow him down. This will allow the back a chance to catch him. As he closes, the defensive back must read the receiver's hands. When the hands come up to receive the ball, the defensive back pulls away one of the receiver's hands while he turns his head toward the ball. He doesn't need to see the ball but he does need to break up the receiver's basket.

Eyes

It is very important for defensive backs to be able to read a receiver's eyes. This is most important when a receiver turns to run deep. The defensive back must turn his back to the quarterback to run with the receiver. At this time the receiver must look for the ball. When the receiver looks, the defensive back must look back at the receiver. If he doesn't look back at the receiver, the receiver may escape the defensive back. The only read for the ball the defensive back has now is the receiver's eyes. A receiver's eyes will always widen as the ball approaches on a deep pattern. At this time the defensive back must lock out the receiver as he looks for the ball or plays the receiver's hands.

Face

The face read is the easiest to teach. When a receiver is one-on-one deep with his back to the quarterback, the defensive back must look at the receiver's face. When the receiver looks for the ball, the defensive back should lock out the receiver and play the ball. This is much the same as reading eyes.

Center of Gravity

When a receiver wants to break a pattern off short, he must drop his center of gravity. We call this breakdown. A defensive back must plant his rear foot and begin driving on the receiver when he reads a breakdown. As the defensive back drives on the receiver's spine, he looks for the receiver's direction of pattern, inside or out. Once he has determined direction of pattern, he then drives on the receiver's upfield shoulder looking for the ball.

Upfield Shoulder

The receiver's upfield shoulder is the shoulder nearest the goal line he is trying to reach. We always want our defensive backs to work for the receiver's upfield shoulder. From the upfield shoulder position he can play any ball thrown. If the ball is thrown ahead of the receiver, he is in perfect position to play the pass. If the ball is thrown short behind the receiver, the defensive back can cut back behind the receiver and take the ball.

Combinations

It is important for defensive backs to be taught receiver combinations. By combinations we refer to common offensive patterns run by two receiver combinations. Two receiver combinations can be:

1. Tight end and flanker.
2. Slotback and wide receiver.
3. The weak side halfback and the wide receiver.
4. Twin sets (two receivers to each side).
5. Trips (three receivers to one side).

It is important that when a defensive back sees an outside receiver moving to the inside the defensive back must realize that the inside receiver is going to make a move to the outside. If the outside receiver runs a deep route, the inside receiver will more than likely run an under pattern to the outside. If the inside receiver runs a deep route, the outside receiver will either run deep to the outside or break back inside under the inside receiver's pattern. Any time the inside receiver runs an out move into an up pattern, the defensive back responsible for flat cover should immediately look to the curl for the outside receiver. Receivers' patterns read by defensive backs save wasting backs covering areas that receivers have left.

Taking on Blockers

Defensive backs must understand when to take on blockers and when to slow-play them. If they are primary run support and blockers show in front of the ball, they must destroy the blockers in a way that forces the ball back inside. If they are secondary run support and the ball with blockers has turned upfield, the defensive back must keep his feet and slow the upfield progress until pursuit arrives. We also teach slip techniques to avoid backs coming out of the backfield to block. Our slip technique has been very effective against option offenses.

Tackling

This has to be worked on in every drill, live or not. Proper position and the right angles to the ball carrier must always be taken. In all drills the coach must demand perfection. It is understood that tackling is what makes good and bad secondaries. Tackling isn't enough. The secondary must be high-speed strikers. We do not tackle, we strike blows.

Locking Off a Receiver

This technique is used when an outside receiver has turned upfield in a one-on-one foot race to the goal line with a defensive back. When the receiver turns to look for the ball, the defensive back turns to look. At this time, the defensive back must step back into the receiver and make contact with his hips. This is not only to screen off the receiver, but the hip contact is most important to keep the receiver from jumping the defensive back for the ball.

Angles

Angles are important because they can save time and steps. If used properly, they can allow a defensive back to close down zones while still covering secondary receivers coming into their area. Angles are most important in closing down on the ball, especially in the open field. Teaching angles is a must to contain the speed of very fast running backs and receivers.

Turning to Run

Knowing when to turn and run with a receiver has to be taught. We work on it in agilities every day. When a receiver has committed to a deep route, it must be read and reacted to at the right time or the defensive back is beaten and must now try to catch the receiver. The defensive back must keep his eyes on the receiver once he has turned to run with him deep to keep the receiver from breaking off the pattern. The defensive back must read only the receiver once he has turned upfield to the outside. He must read his face, eyes and hands once they are running stride for stride down the sideline. The defensive back looks for the ball only when the receiver looks.

Strip

A defensive back must try to take at least one of the receiver's hands away from making a catch when he makes contact going to the ball. It is preferred to have the defensive back try to take both arms away from the ball at contact when he is screened off. This is not always possible. It is, however, possible to strip the receiver of at least one arm on every pattern. The defensive back must work to the ball and try to knock it down. When screened by the receiver, good, hard contact plus one arm being pulled away will break up most pass completions if the defensive back is close to the catch.

Play Through Receivers

Defensive backs should attack through a receiver as if his point of contact is two yards the other side of the receiver. This makes his point of contact much more effective. He must drive through a receiver to meet the ball. Any time he makes a move in front of a receiver, he must at least bump him on the way by. This will break the receiver's concentration in case the ball is misjudged and the receiver has a play on it.

Adjustment Reactions

When a defensive adjustment must be made due to offensive formation, shifts or motion, the defensive secondary must be able to adjust without looking lost or panicked. These adjustments are usually only a few steps unless the strong safety is chasing motion. The secondary must never look surprised or disoriented by anything the offense may throw at them. A defensive back who must make a position change must make it as smoothly and confidently as he can. To look confused or lost can cause panic and missed assignments.

4

FORMATIONS

Formations can tell a secondary a lot about offensive intentions before the ball is snapped. Good scouting reports can help with defensive cover calls and overall secondary reaction to certain key offensive plays. Secondaries must be schooled to handle any and all offensive sets. The teaching of formations by run-first sets (Diagrams 4:1-4:10), run- or pass-sets (Diagrams 4:11-4:20), and pass-first sets (Diagrams 4:21-4:28) can cut down on confusion and make for a strong secondary.

Formations Run First

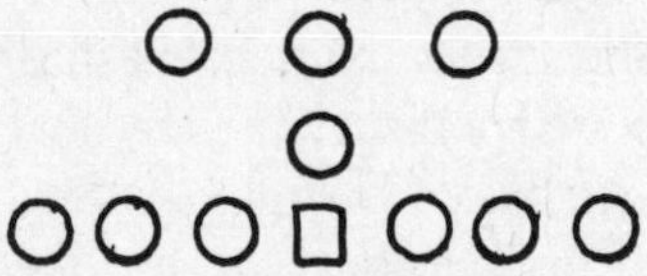

O O O
O
O O O □ O O O

Diagram 4:1. Full House.

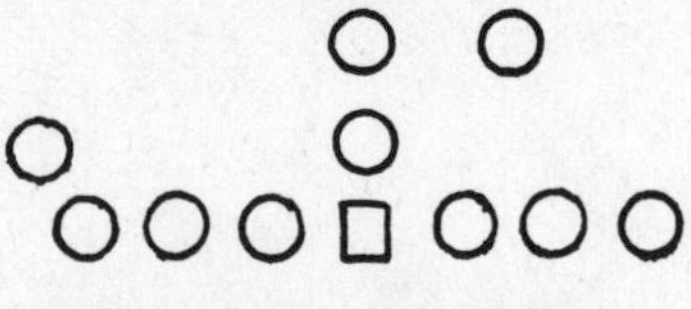

O   O
O   O
O O O □ O O O

Diagram 4:2. Weak Wing.

O   O
O   O
O O O □ O O O

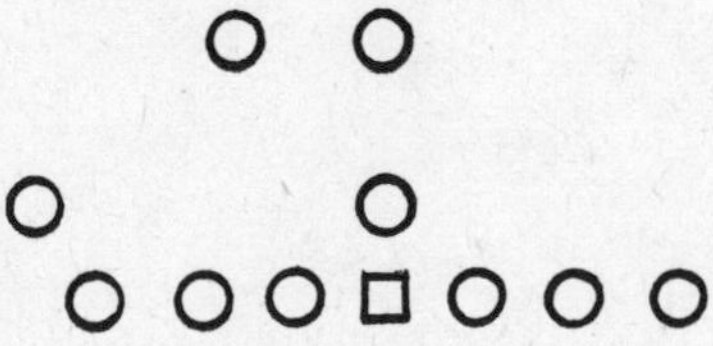

Diagram 4:3. Strong Wing.

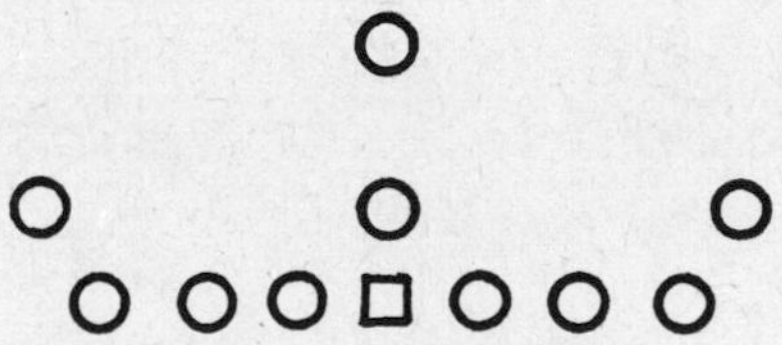

Diagram 4:4. Double Wing.

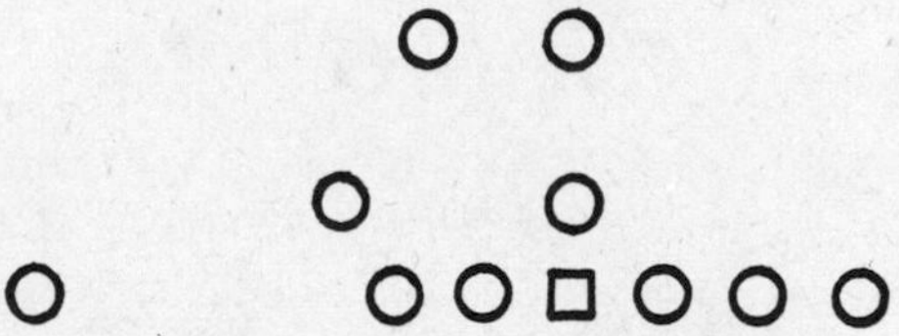

Diagram 4:5. Strong Slot.

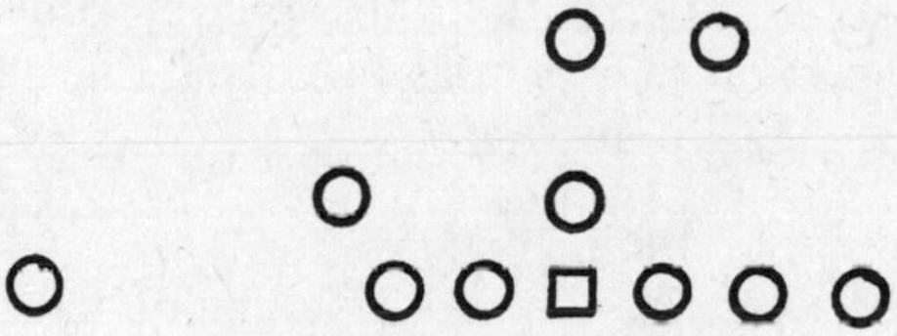

Diagram 4:6. Weak Slot.

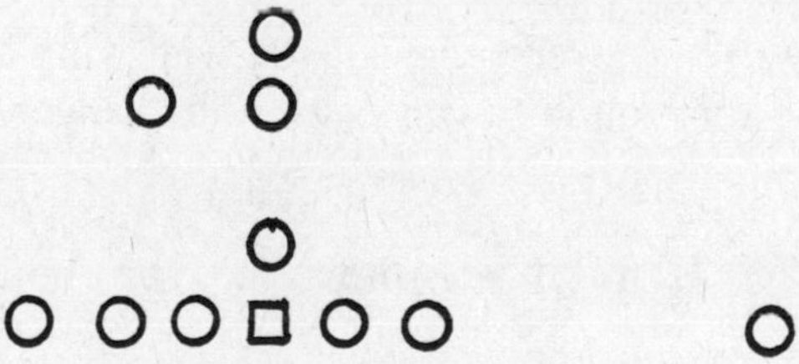

Diagram 4:7. Strong Power I.

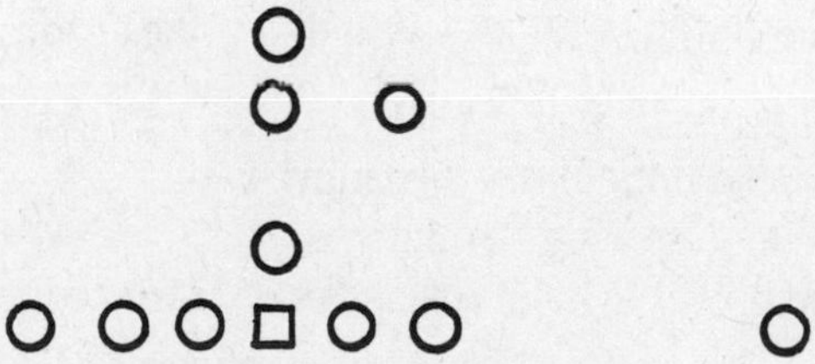

Diagram 4:8. Weak Power I.

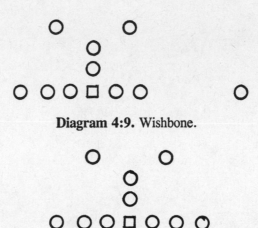

Diagram 4:9. Wishbone.

Diagram 4:10. Tight Bone.

Although these formations are run most of the time, they are used for play-action passes on short yardage and goal line situations. These formations have definite strengths:

1. Strong inside the tackles.
2. Can attack inside the tackles going either way.
3. Good for counter and traps.
4. Can run multi-back deception.
5. Good middle power.
6. Easy to run reverses or counter with wing or slot.
7. Good for motion to cause strength changes.

Formations for Run or Passes

These formations allow for both run strengths and passing strength. The passing strengths come from the three quick receivers. The running strengths come from spreading the defense out and still having a two-back offense. The strengths of these formations are:

1. Strong run or pass to the two-receiver side.
2. Balanced enough to run either way.
3. Excellent passing formations.
4. Good power to back strength side. I formation can run either way.

5. Good for sweeps and wide plays.
6. Offensive backs are in good position to be used in the passing game.

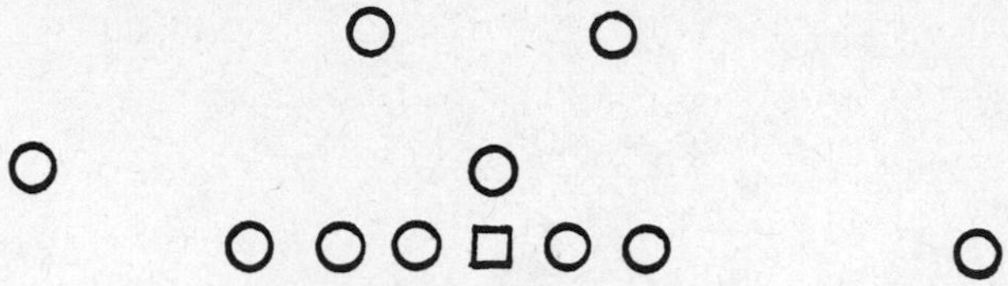

Diagram 4:11. Split pro.

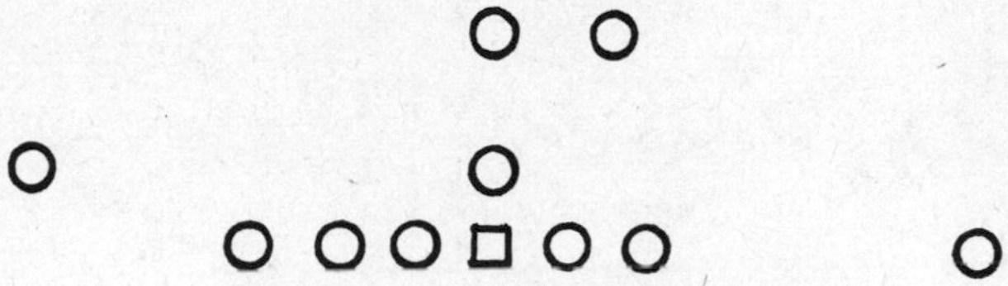

Diagram 4:12. Weak pro.

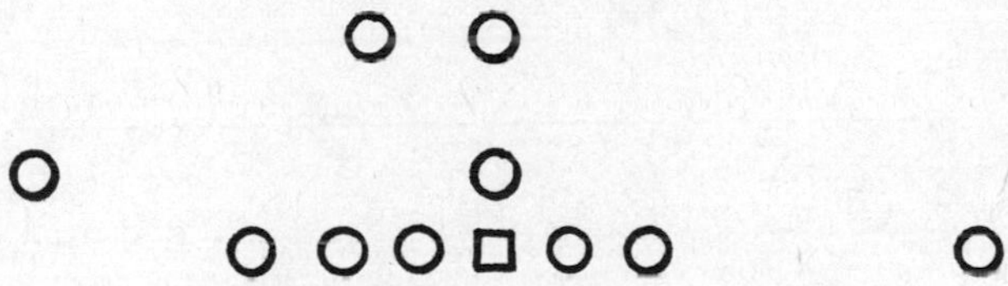

Diagram 4:13. Strong pro.

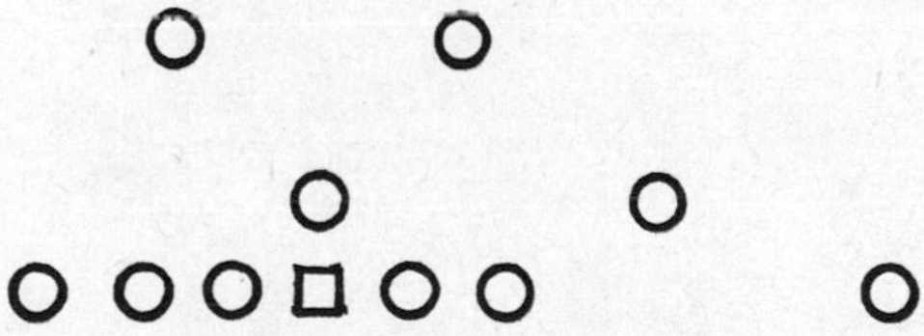

Diagram 4:14. Split slot.

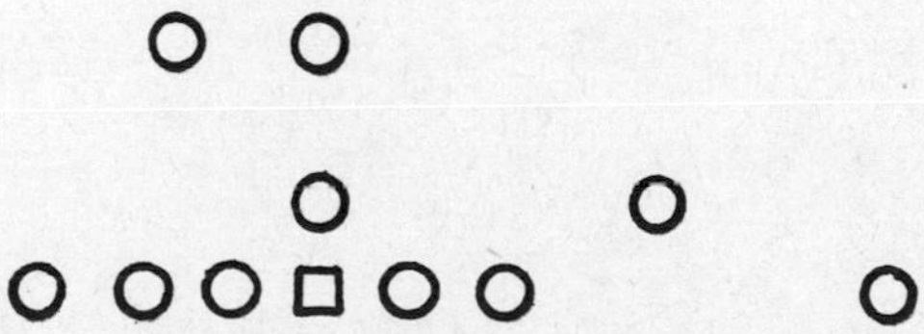

Diagram 4:15. Weak slot.

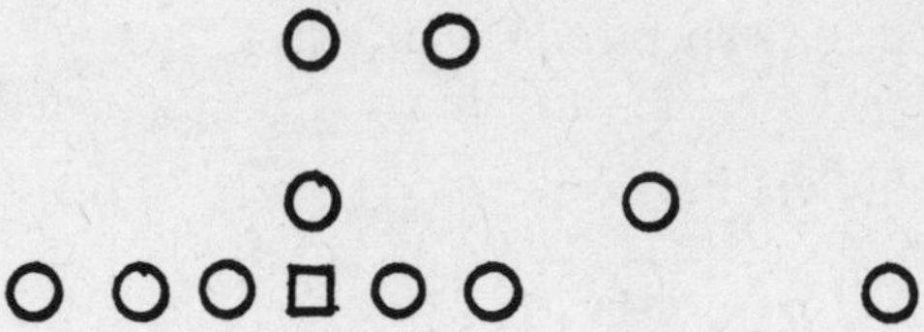

Diagram 4:16. Strong slot.

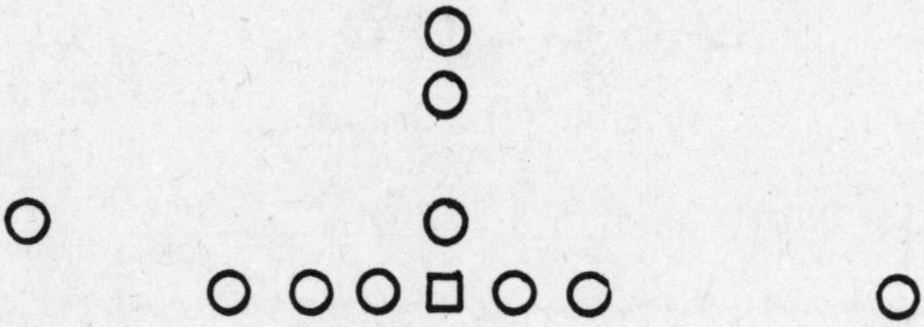

Diagram 4:17. Pro I.

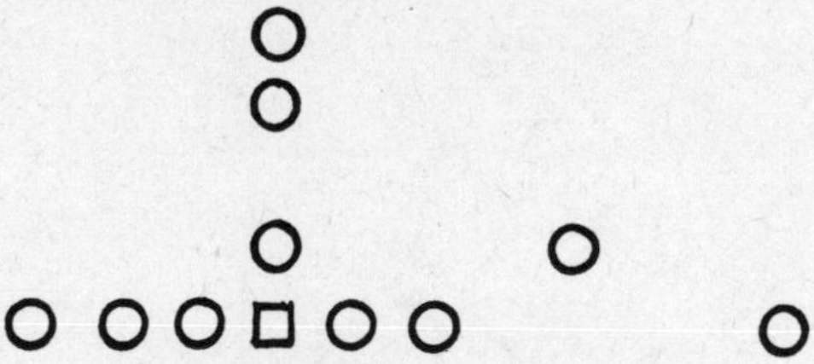

Diagram 4:18. Slot I

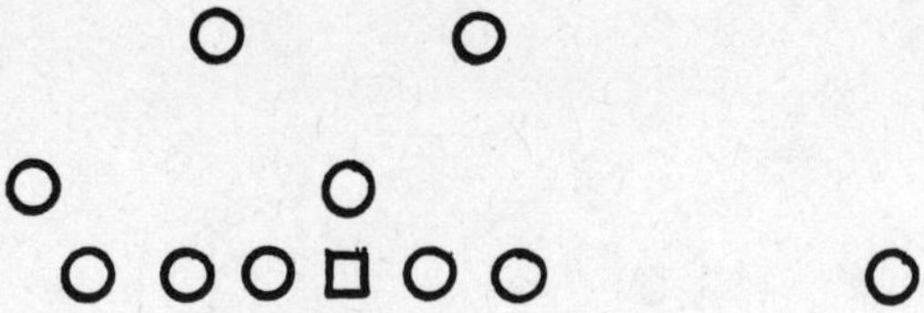

Diagram 4:19. Split wing.

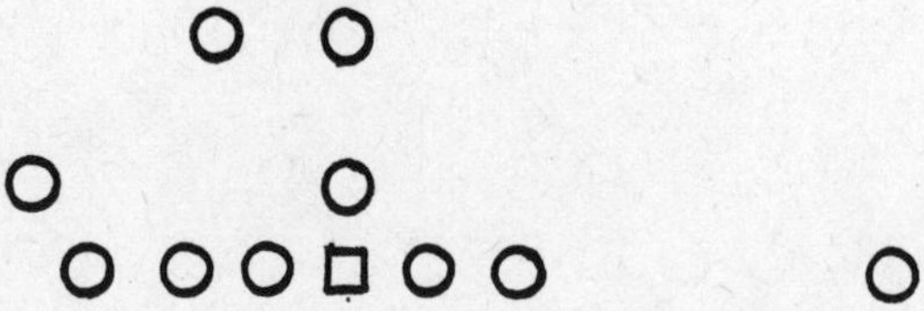

Diagram 4:20. Strong wing.

Formations Which Are Pass First

There are many four-receiver formations and possible five-receiver formations. They are mostly pass. The reason for this is that they have no deception and are easily keyed. There also is no lead back to clear the hole. It does provide for strong outside blocking from receivers for sweeps. The strengths of these formations are:

1. They require special defensive covers.
2. Easy to beat a blitz with quick, short passes into the areas where the linebackers have left.
3. Easy to flood zones with receivers.
4. With shotguns, the passer gets a longer look at the defense.
5. With shotguns, the passer is in a good position to throw quickly.
6. Can run good reverses.

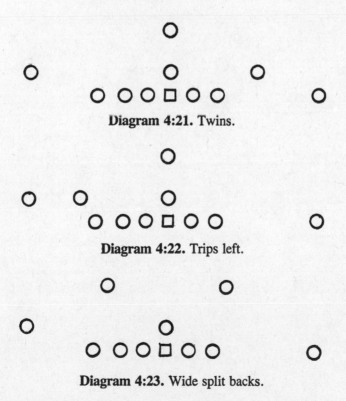

Diagram 4:21. Twins.

Diagram 4:22. Trips left.

Diagram 4:23. Wide split backs.

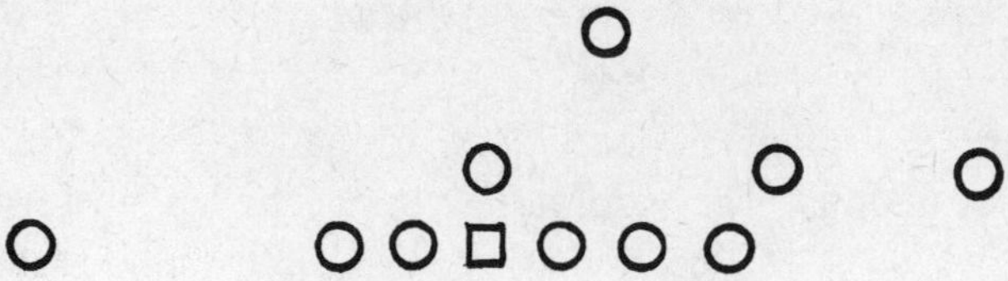

Diagram 4:24. Trips back right.

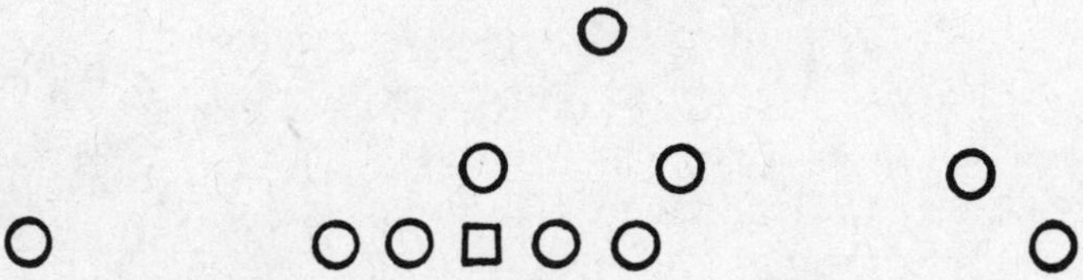

Diagram 4:25. Trips set back strong.

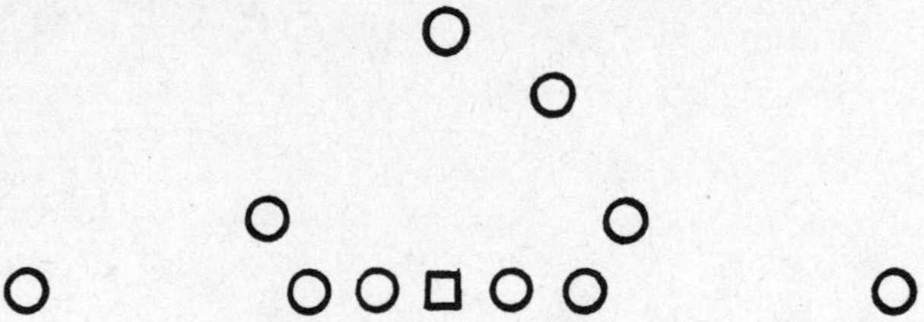

Diagram 4:26. Shotgun twins.

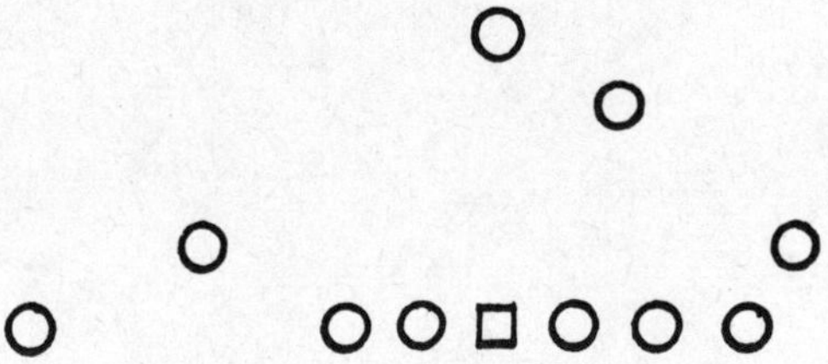

Diagram 4:27. Shotgun twins.

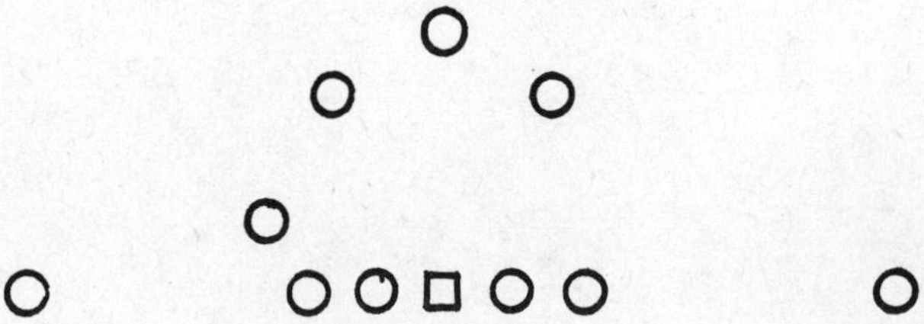

Diagram 4:28. Shotgun.

In defensive football today it is very difficult to say that the defensive secondary call in the huddle will be the same defense we will be playing at the snap of the ball. The biggest factor determining secondary calls is formations. In today's multi-offensive attacks most adjustments are made with the secondary. We have in certain games changed our covers as many as four times from the time we left the huddle to the time the ball was snapped. The biggest reason for the changes on the defenses is formation changes by the offense. The offense could come out in a formation that our secondary would not cover well. This could cause a change. The offense could shift to a different formation which would cause a change. The offense could motion to a different set which could cause a change, or they could do all of the aforementioned. All of these adjustments must be made quickly and simply.

5

COVERS

In Chapter 5, I will cover many formations in drawing form to show our alignments and adjustments before the snap of the ball. The actual playing of these covers and the techniques used will be discussed later in other chapters.

Our covers are simple if taught in the proper order. Never try to teach any more than Cover 1 until Cover 1 is fully understood. Once all the techniques of Cover 1 are understood, Covers 2, 3, 5, 8 and 9 have, for the most part, already been taught.

Cover 1 will get you through most ball games because it's a reading zone. If you read well, you will always have support where you need it. Have your lower divisions teach Cover 1 until your athletes know every technique. Without knowing it, they have set in motion the teaching of Covers 2, 3, 5, 8 and 9, leaving the varsity to teach 4, 6, and 7. Techniques for Cover 1 will be described fully in the next chapter.

Cover 1

Cover 1 is a reading zone. If strong action is read (Diagrams 5:1-5:2 and 5:4), the strong safety attacks the run or covers the flat against the pass. Corners and free safety go to deep thirds. If weak action is the read (Diagram 5:3), the weak corner attacks the run or covers the flat against a pass to the weak side. The free safety covers deep outside. The strong safety goes to deep middle and the strong corner covers outside third. Any backfield action other than the quarterback and one or more backs attacking the weak side is considered strong.

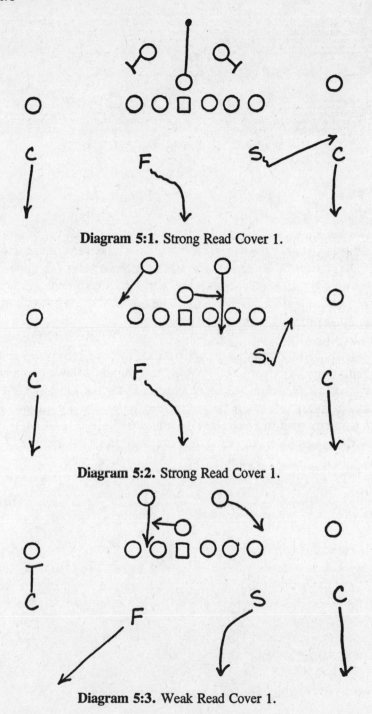

Diagram 5:1. Strong Read Cover 1.

Diagram 5:2. Strong Read Cover 1.

Diagram 5:3. Weak Read Cover 1.

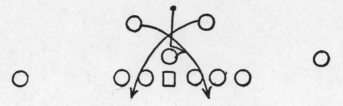

Diagram 5:4. Strong Read Cover 1.

Cover 2

Cover 2 is a reading zone. The only difference in Cover 2 is that the free safety will attack the weak side run or cover the weak flat against the pass (Diagram 5:6). Everyone else in the defense stays the same. The reason we have Cover 2 is that a few times in a game we will have a Cover 1 called and the offense will come out with the weak side of the formation to the wide side of the field. If the receivers take a wide enough split so that the free safety feels he would have trouble covering the wide receiver if he ran a corner pattern, the free safety will change the weak side to a Cover 2. This allows the corner to stay with the wide receiver on weak action. All other positions stay the same as Cover 1. Cover 2 is between the weak corner and the free safety. The difference in the cover is shown in Diagrams 5:5 and 5:6.

We like to keep our free safety deep as much as possible. There would be no change in either cover if strong side action shows.

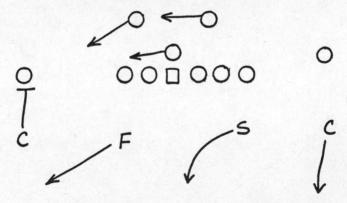

Diagram 5:5. Cover 1 Weak Action.

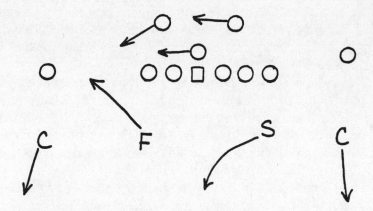

Diagram 5:6. Cover 2 Weak Action. Note: Free safety will cheat up if two is called.

Cover 3

For all intents and purposes Cover 3 is a three-deep umbrella zone with many possibilities underneath the umbrella. We use Cover 3 against power sets, slot sets, wing sets, most motion and in most trips and twin sets. We like having the deep areas covered at all times. We can move our strong safety to the weak side if our scouting reports so dictate. However, we have seldom done this. When we set a Cover 3, we always want to slant away from it. The three gives us the extra man to the strong side so we slant back to the weak.

The toughest formations to deal with for the run first offenses are the power sets (Diagrams 5:7-5:14). Against power sets we use our Cover 3. Cover 3 is a three-deep zone with our strong safety playing like a linebacker. We would use Cover 3 against most teams which run the following sets. We would place our strong safety right in the middle of the formation strength against these sets unless scouting reports told us different.

The free safety is influenced by field position, hash marks, down and distance, plus scouting reports. However, we start his alignment at 15 yards deep and in the middle of the formation, not only over the football. A corner with a tight end aligns three yards outside the tight end and five yards off the ball. Corners with a split end align one yard outside and six yards deep. The strong safety has many positions to line up in Cover 3. However, his basic rule is three yards off the ball with no deep responsibility. Cover 3 is our most versatile cover. We run many kinds of Cover 3 as you will see.

The reason for different Cover 3s and cover changes before the ball is snapped is that we want to be in the best possible defense for the offensive formation when the ball is snapped. Even when you're in the best possible defense, it has to be played by all eleven players. It requires good coaching to be able to get eleven people to respond quickly to a linebacker's or free safety's defensive changes.

Many formations used by an opponent can be covered with three or four of our covers, so scouting dictates whether we should use a good run cover or pass cover for a particular formation.

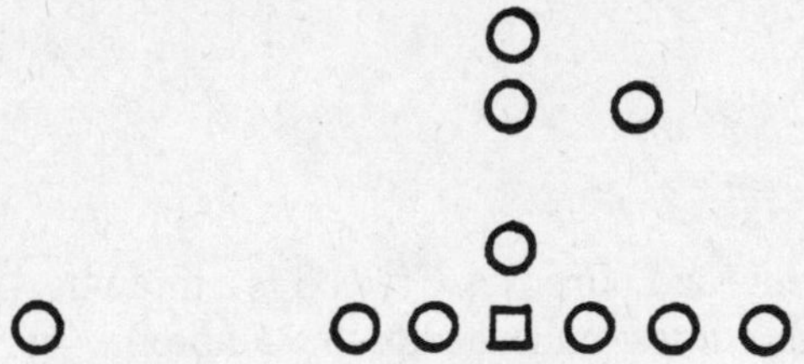

Diagram 5:7. Power I right.

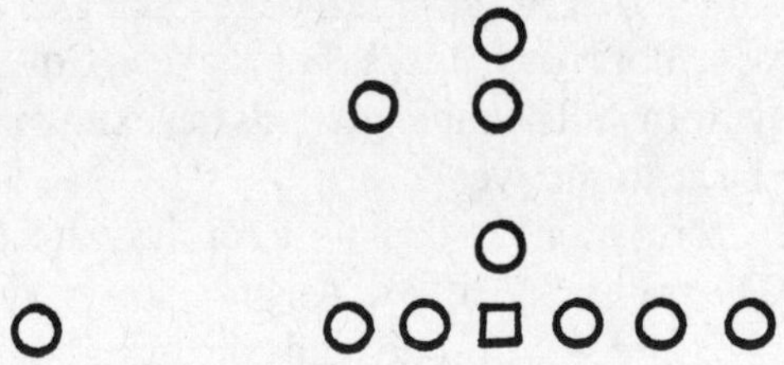

Diagram 5:8. Power I left.

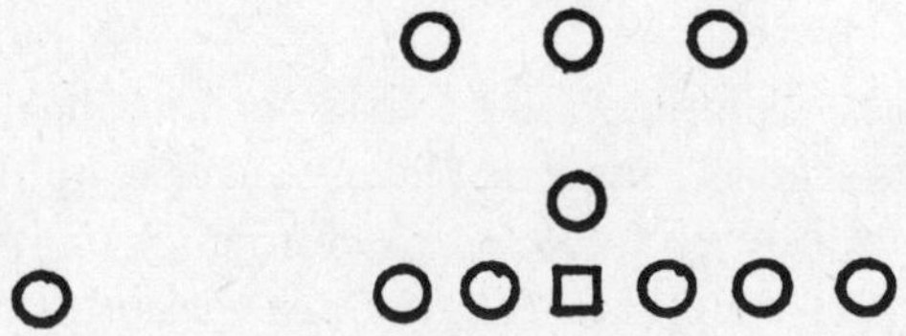

Diagram 5:9. Full house.

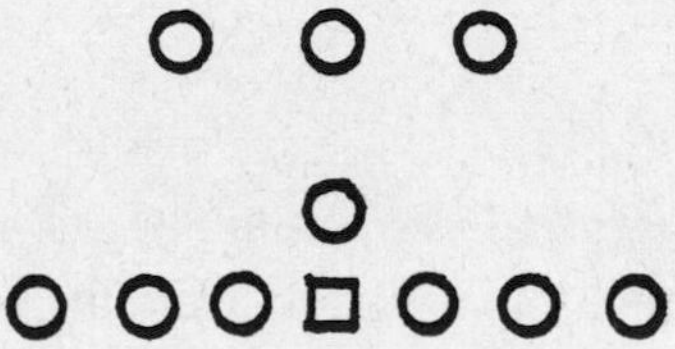

Diagram 5:10. Full house double-tight.

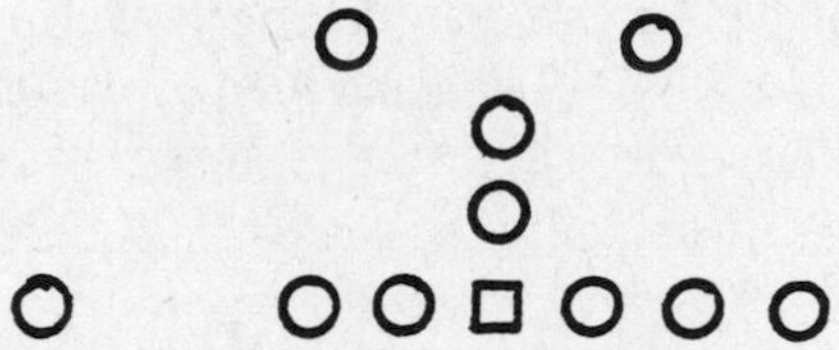

Diagram 5:11. Wishbone.

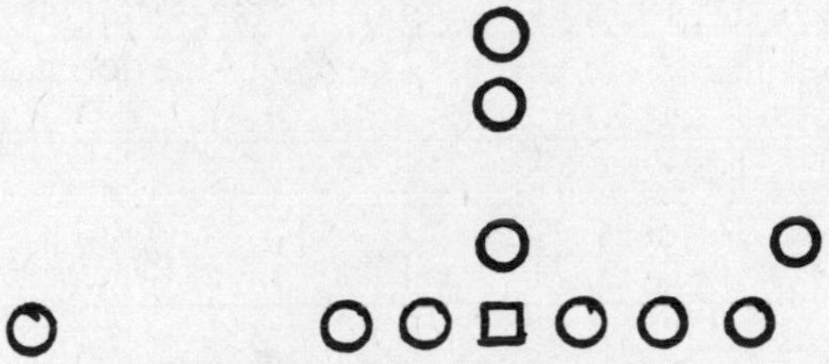

Diagram 5:12. Wing set.

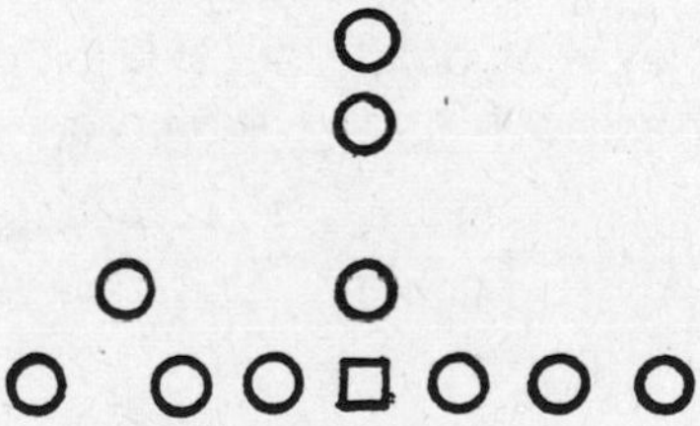

Diagram 5:13. Tight slot set.

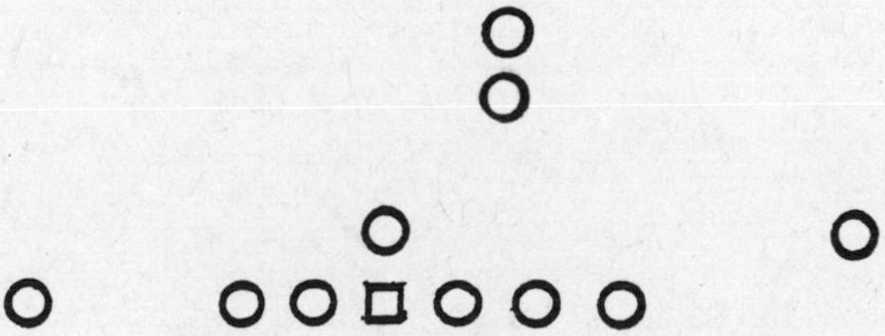

Diagram 5:14. Offset stacks.

Cover 4

We run three cover fours. *Straight cover four* is man across the board. The free safety picks up the back out to the weak side. The strong safety has the tight end or slotback man-for-man. Another Cover 4 is called *4 combo*. In 4 combo the strong safety plays the tight end or slot man-for-man and the corners play man-for-man on their receivers. The big difference is that the free safety is playing zone. He is free to help on the ball. The last Cover 4 is *goal line* and it involves some combinations in reads. We will discuss it later.

Cover 5

Cover 5 is the same as Cover 1 for the secondary; the difference here is that both ends are crashing. The rest of the defense plays regular.

Cover 6

Cover 6 is a combination zone and man-for-man. It is a good change-up from our Cover 3 against a slot. It is designed to close the slot off.

In Cover 6 we play zone on the slot side and man on the tight end side (Diagrams 5:15 and 5:16). The weak corner has the tight end

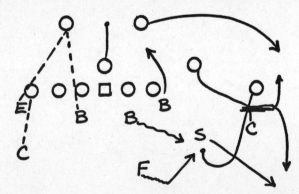

Diagram 5:15. Corner will release an up pattern after making solid contact on the receiver. This will enable him to pick up any screen or swing back to his side. The strong safety has the up while the free safety and the weak backer will take the curl.

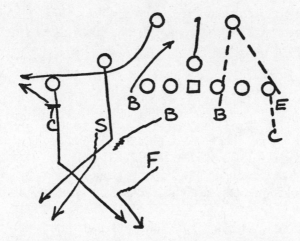

Diagram 5:16. The free safety has post, strong safety has the corner, corner back has back out, and strong backer plays curl to short post.

man-for-man, while the weak backer and strong end have a combination man on the back to their side. If the back swings or runs to the flat, the strong end takes him all the way. If the back circles up inside, or runs a seam route in the middle, the weak backer has him. On the slot side the free safety takes any post move or curl. The corner plays the out hard, while the strong safety plays any deep outside move. The strong side backer plays any curl or inside pattern.

Cover 7

Cover 7 must be run in special situations. It is a five-under-2 deep zone. It is very good against many passing and running attacks. However, it can be costly if run too often against a team that can get 3 receivers deep quickly.

The five-under, like all our zone defenses, builds off our Cover 1. We try hard not to do anything, technique-wise, in any of our zones that we don't do in Cover 1. In this way, when we have taught Cover 1, we have taught most of the techniques for all our zones.

Cover 8

Cover 8 is a predetermined roll to X. X is the weak side wide receiver. In all of our other zone covers we read back action to determine our roll, but in Cover 8 we roll to the weak side no matter what the backs do. This gives us a double cover on X with the flat covered by the corner if anything shows out there.

Cover 9

Cover 9 is just like Cover 8 only it is a predetermined strong side roll. Again, in this cover it makes no difference where the backs go since we will roll the secondary to the strong side. Again, the rest of the defense would either play straight or slant away from the roll in Covers 8 and 9.

We have one other predetermined roll which we call *Sting Number*. In offenses where they move their best receiver from X to Z, to a slot and so on, we will just sting the receiver's number. *Example:* If number 81 is their best receiver, we will call "Sting 81." No matter where 81 lines up on offense, we will sting him with a roll. The roll call for the rest of the defense will be made after the formation is set. The free safety makes a call of Cover 8 or 9 and the linebackers will make a call, if we are slanting, which is opposite the roll call.

6

READS AND KEYS IN COVER 1

Cover 1, as explained in the preceding chapter, is a reading zone. It reads flow of the backs to determine which way the secondary will roll.

Cover 1, when taught completely, gives your players every technique they need to play Covers 2, 3, 5, 8 and 9. In order to play the corner up on wear action, both corners must be taught the short zone technique. Cover 2 weak action is the same as Cover 1 strong action, just a different safety inverts. So you teach both safeties to invert when you teach Cover 1. Cover 3 is a predetermined invert with the strong safety lining up where he's supposed to run to in Cover 1 strong action. Cover 5 is a Cover 1. All deep zone techniques are the same for all of the covers. So by doing a good job with Cover 1, you are teaching many other covers.

Basic Cover 1 Rules, Weak Action

A. Corners and free safety key remaining backs for flow weak or strong.

1. We start our athletes off reading only for weak action. We tell them if it doesn't read weak, we always go strong.

B. The free safety must always check the distance of the weak side split to be sure he can beat the football to the corner.

C. The weak corner on weak side action must always make contact with the receiver and force him to the inside (Diagram 6:1).

1. If the receiver tries to go to the outside, the weak corner must drive him to the sideline. No quick releases.
2. The minute the weak corner makes contact with the wide receiver, he looks in the backfield for a back out to his side.
3. On an inside move by the receiver, the weak corner will go with him until someone crosses his face to the outside. At that point he will release the receiver and move with the outside threat. This is a technique which must be drilled. The short zone is no place to guard grass. A good drill for this is described in Chapter 10 (Diagram 10:27).

D. The free safety, moving to the outside third to cover the wide receiver, must, after he gets his weak read, find the wide receiver.

1. If the wide receiver is coming inside, the free safety will set his hips to the inside five yards from the receiver and move inside with him until someone crosses his face to the outside deep (Diagrams 6:1 and 6:2). This helps to close the zones. A defensive back should never run by a receiver crossing a zone opposite his action without checking the quarterback.

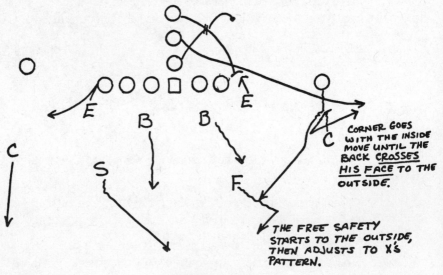

Diagram 6:1

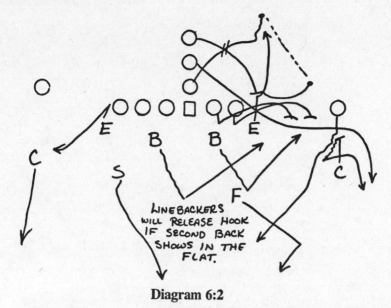

LINEBACKERS WILL RELEASE HOOK IF SECOND BACK SHOWS IN THE FLAT.

Diagram 6:2

2. If the receiver has made an outside move, the free safety must fly to the outside to protect against the bomb (Diagram 6:3). He must take his deep angle and then check the quarterback for a drop pass in the weak side hole.
3. If no one is out in the flat, the weak corner can help in the hole by taking the proper angle (Diagram 6:4).

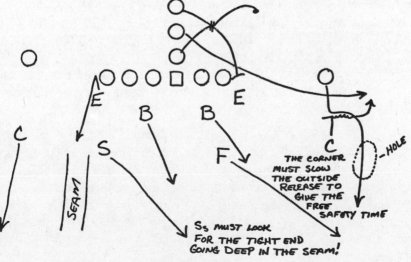

THE CORNER MUST SLOW THE OUTSIDE RELEASE TO GIVE THE FREE SAFETY TIME

Ss MUST LOOK FOR THE TIGHT END GOING DEEP IN THE SEAM!

Diagram 6:3

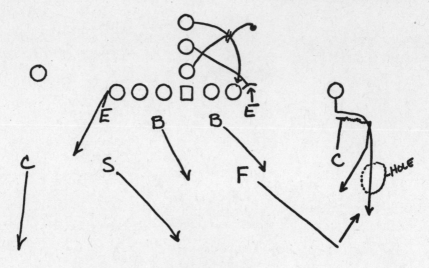

Diagram 6:4

E. The strong safety reads the tight end first for blockdown or release. The strong safety reads always for his first two backward steps.

1. If the tight end blocks down, he quickly looks in the backfield for flow. If flow is away, he will retreat to the deep middle, cheating to the tight end side and looking for the tight end for a curl. The strong safety is responsible to help on any inside deep pattern.

2. If the tight end releases, the strong safety looks into the backfield for flow. If flow is away, he retreats to the deep middle looking for the tight end as he goes (Diagram 6:5). He is responsible for any inside deep patterns.

3. If the tight end breaks to the outside away from him, the strong safety now looks for Z on an inside route (Diagram 6:6).

F. The action in Cover 1 weak side is much the same against the run. If the weak side corner reads weak side run, he must make contact with the receiver, force him inside and close the split (Diagram 6:7). The split is the distance the receiver has moved the defensive back from the tackle on his side. This split must be closed down because it provides a large running lane and too much room for our linebackers to cover. The corner must take on the lead blocker and at the very worst, turn the play inside.

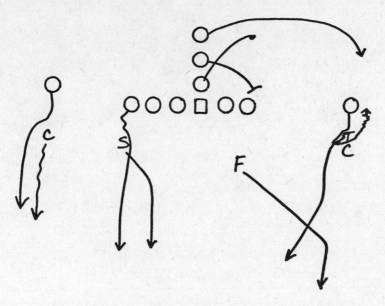

Diagram 6:5

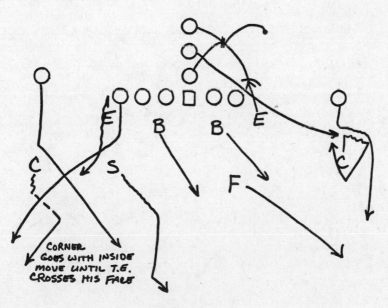

CORNER
GOES WITH INSIDE
MOVE UNTIL T.E.
CROSSES HIS FACE

Diagram 6:6

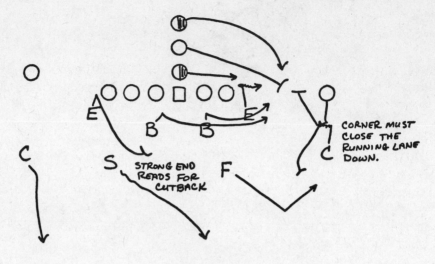

Diagram 6:7

1. The corner is responsible for the pitch man on option.
2. The corner must close down on any running play to the weak side. On power plays he must close tight and look for the back to bounce outside if the hole is jammed (Diagram 6:8).

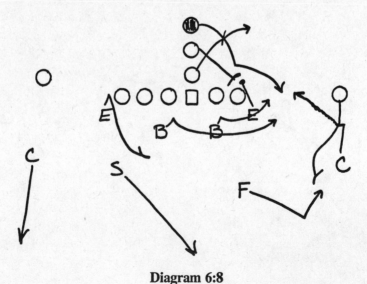

Diagram 6:8

Cover 1 Rules, Strong Action

A. Corners and free safety read is back action. Any action other than the quarterback and a back going to the weak side is read as strong action. Strong back action is shown six different ways in Diagram 6:9.

B. It is possible to get caught in a strong roll and have the offense bootleg back to the weak side. They could run the bootleg off weak action as well. The key to any type of bootleg in Cover 1 is not to try to change the cover. At the snap of the ball the whole defense must play the same cover. The defense will shift with the quarterback action.

C. When strong action is read as pass, the corners and free safety go to the deep zones. Corners play the outside deep zones and the free safety plays the deep middle (Diagram 6:10).

1. The strong corner will play any outside move by the side receiver and look for the tight end in a deep route. He can play the first outside move for three steps; if the ball is not thrown in that time, he must release to any deep route being run by the tight end. If the tight end turns inside or breaks off a short route, the corner can stay with the wide receiver. If on the three-step read by the corner the quarterback throws the ball, the corner can play the ball and ignore any tight end deep route. Due to the angles, the corner can play the wide receiver for at least three steps before releasing. Time and distance are real factors here. If the tight end is challenging deep and the wide receiver is loafing off, the corner would have to release the out to the strong safety and get deep (Diagram 6:11).

2. If the wide receiver runs an inside route, the corner must go with him, reading for anyone to *cross his face*. If nobody is going to the outside, he can go with the receiver. If there is a receiver crossing to the outside, the corner can go three steps with the inside route to see if the ball is thrown. If the ball is not thrown to the inside route within the three steps, the inside receiver will run into the safety before the ball can get to him, if it's not in the air by his third inside step. If the ball is not thrown inside, the corner can release and pick up any outside route being run deep (Diagram 6:12).

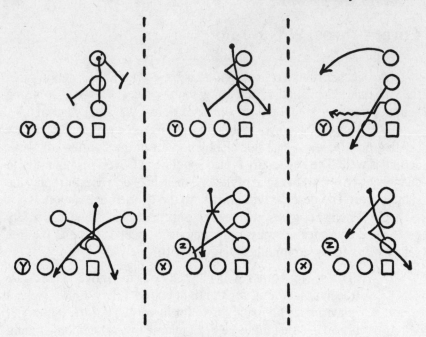

Diagram 6:9

Diagram 6:10

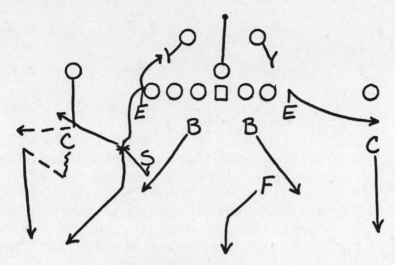

Diagram 6:11

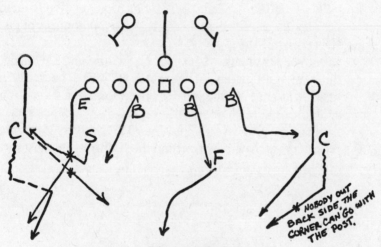

Diagram 6:12

3. The free safety must stay in the middle and flow with the quarterback's head and shoulders. By flow, we mean open his hips to the side the quarterback is looking, but do not break in that direction. He must stay in the middle, until he sees the quarterback take his lead hand off the ball. He then must get into a collision course with the inside route the quarterback is throwing to.

D. The strong safety reads for strong action in a different way. His first read is the tight end.

1. If the tight end blocks down, he starts to attack the line of scrimmage as he looks into the backfield for flow.
2. If flow is to the weak side, the strong safety will retreat to deep middle.
3. If flow is to the strong side, the strong safety will attack the line of scrimmage. His angle will depend on the angle of the offensive backs. If the backs are both attacking anywhere on the strong side from the off-tackle hole to the center, the strong safety will keep an outside-in angle on the ball carrier and step up behind the strong end. If the play is at the off-tackle hole, the strong safety will play one yard behind the strong end and read inside (Diagram 6:13). If the ball shows inside, he will tackle it. If the strong end closes the hole off, the strong safety will be in good position to attack with an inside-out angle on the ball when it bounces outside (Diagram 6:14).
4. If both backs or either back takes a flat angle to the outside, the safety will flatten out and attack the widest back with an inside-out angle to the outside. If option shows the strong safety has the pitch man in this defense, he must, as soon as he reads a wide play, look for the wide receiver. If the wide receiver is coming down on him, the strong safety must try to

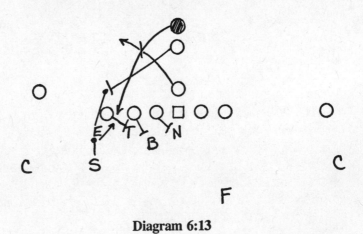

Diagram 6:13

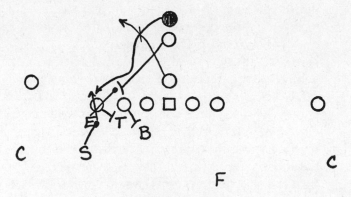

Diagram 6:14

beat the block across the line of scrimmage or he must cock his inside arm and attack the receiver's outside shoulder (Diagram 6:15). The strong safety must close the split side down, maintain the outside and force the play in if he can't make the tackle.

5. If the tight end releases from the line of scrimmage, the strong safety will read for backfield flow as he continues to retreat. If flow is away, he will retreat to the middle as he looks for the tight end, or wide receiver.

6. If the tight end releases from the line of scrimmage and the safety reads strong action, the safety looks quickly and takes three steps for a quick pass to the tight end. If the ball is not

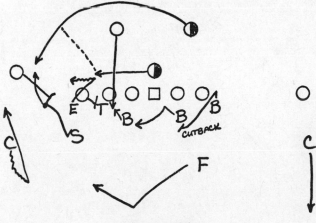

Diagram 6:15

thrown, the safety will head for the flat, looking for the wide receiver. If the wide receiver breaks to the outside, the safety must get in front of him (Diagram 6:16).

7. As the strong safety breaks outside to the flat, he looks at the wide receiver. If the wide receiver is coming inside, the safety will slow down and try to fill the seam between the corner and safety until someone crosses his face, trying to get to the flat (Diagram 6:17). If the wide receiver is coming inside and the tight end releases down the line of scrimmage, the strong safety will react slowly to the line release of the tight end until he turns up. The safety will try to stall in the seam to force the wide receiver into the safety (Diagram 6:18).

8. Many teams will run tight end look patterns as part of a veer option. If the safety covers the tight end, they pitch. If the strong safety takes the pitch man, they throw the look into the tight end. We look at it this way: our safety is to look at the tight end release. If the release is an outside release, our safety will attack the tight end. If we hit the tight end hard enough, we can destroy his block, if he is a blocker, and knock him off a pass route if he is to be a receiver. We figure

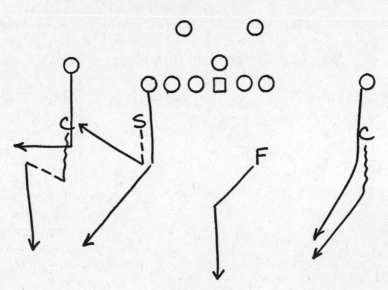

Diagram 6:16

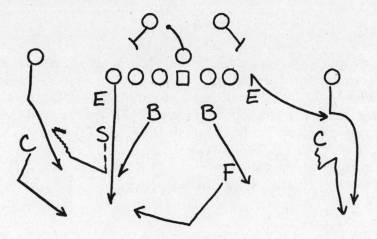

Diagram 6:17

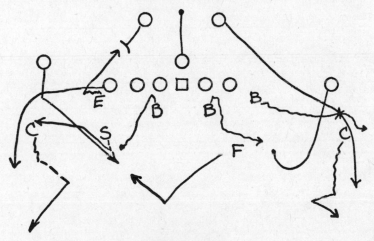

Diagram 6:18

a completed pass is worth a minimum of 12 yards. So we play the tight end first. Also, it is very difficult for the play to be a consistent gainer. If a team can consistently move five yards at a crack, it's time to change covers. This is our basic Cover 1. This cover is what we build all our zone covers on. If we can play Cover 1 well, we can control most offenses. The athletes must believe in this cover, and all other zones will be easy to teach because the zone principles will not change.

SUMMARY

We do not go to a zone and play the ball. We go to a zone, read the receiver combinations, find the nearest receiver, jump on him, and then look for the ball. We try at all times to close the splits of wide people on runs and close down the zone seams on pass. Many steps can be saved in zones if angles are taught and used. DEFENSIVE SECONDARIES NEVER GO HALF-SPEED TO THE BALL in practice. This is the worst habit that can exist in pass defense. Half-speed means your feet are not moving. This is a disaster in the making.

7

COVERS 2, 3, 5, 8 AND 9

Cover 2 Rules, Weak Action

Cover 2 is a free safety call only. It can be made by the coach for a weak side change-up. However, it is basically a fail-safe device. We like to keep our free safety in the deep zones where we can use his talents to get us the football. There are, however, game situations that could put our defense at a disadvantage if we tried to play Cover 1 regularly. The rules for a Cover 2 weak side action do not change on the strong side from Cover 1.

The difference between Cover 1 and Cover 2 is weak side action only. The call is made by the free safety when he feels he could not cover the wide receiver to the weak side, if the receiver were to run a flag pattern with weak action. If the wide receiver had the wide side of the field and took a very wide split, the free safety would change the weak side cover to Cover 2. In Cover 2 the free safety covers the flat on weak action. If weak action shows, the free safety will play much as the strong safety plays strong action.

A. If the backs drive into the line on a power play from the off-tackle hole to the center on the weak side, the free safety will come up and attack the ball from the outside in.

B. If the backs attack the off-tackle hole with a power play, the free safety closes to within one yard off the outside backer. If the back breaks inside, the safety will attack the ball. If the back breaks outside, the free safety is in position to make the play (Diagram 7:1).

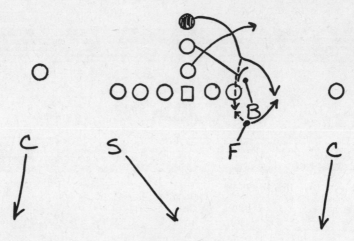

Diagram 7:1

C. On pass read to the weak side, the free safety starts to the flat and looks for the wide receiver. The advantage of the weak side Cover 2 is that the free safety doesn't have to look for a tight end.

  1. If the wide receiver comes inside, the free safety will try to stall him off on a slant as long as the back to his side doesn't cross his face.
  2. If the back does cross his face, the free safety must go with the back.
  3. If the wide receiver breaks to the outside on a sideline, the free safety must get in the line of flight of the ball to the outside (Diagram 7:2).

Cover 2 is designed to protect our defense from wide splits by the X receiver in an attempt to beat our safety to the corner. It also gives us a change-up to play the outside running game, especially the option play.

Cover 3

Cover 3 is used in many ways in our defensive schemes. We have several Cover 3s that we can run. These different Cover 3s allow us to disguise our defense and confuse offensive reads.

A. In all our Cover 3s we play a three-deep umbrella zone. Both corners play the deep outside zone while the free safety plays deep middle.

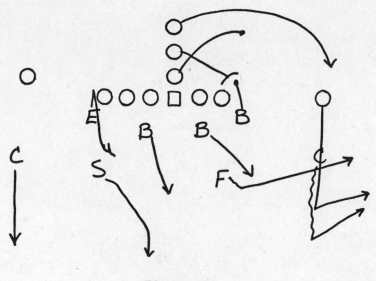

Diagram 7:2

B. In Cover 3 we make all our changes with our strong safety and ends.

C. We have six Cover 3 calls.

1. Cover 3
2. Cover 3 Man
3. Cover 3 Switch
4. Cover 3 Sting
5. Cover 3 Blood
6. Cover 3 Cheat

D. Cover 3 is a predetermined strong side zone. We do not read any backs to determine our zone. All reads and keys for Cover 1 strong side action are the same for Cover 3, even if the back action is weak.

E. We use Cover 3 against most slot sets. We cheat the strong safety up to three yards off the ball. He is to read the slot the same as a tight end (Diagram 7:3).

F. The weak corner against a slot has to play the tight end five yards off the ball and three yards outside. He must read for block down by the tight end. If he blocks down, the corner must come up quickly to help against the run. The free safety will float to the weak side looking for the tight end to escape into a pass pattern (Diagram 7:4).

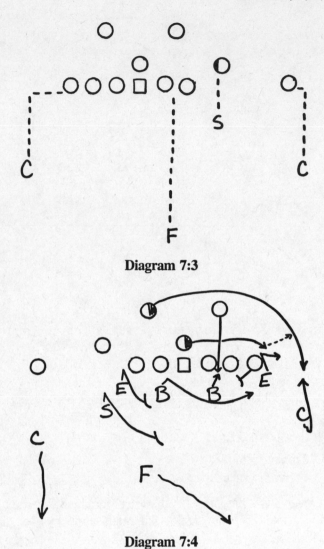

Diagram 7:3

Diagram 7:4

G. If the tight end releases, the corner has to go with him. This allows the weak side tackle to take an outside lane. The weak tackle now has outside contained (Diagram 7:5).

Cover 3 Man

A. Cover 3 man has the three-deep umbrella zone, but we play our strong safety man-for-man on the tight end or the slot back, if the offensive set is a slot.

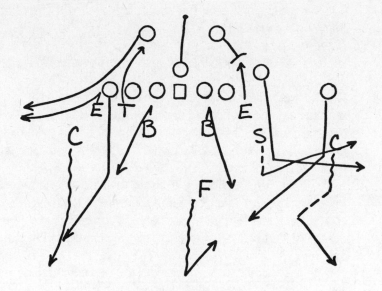

Diagram 7:5

B. We will run this cover to stop a team that likes to throw to the tight end from play action or quick look-ins. We also run it against slot sets where teams throw to the slot under zone covers or on stop patterns. It takes the second receiver out of strong side patterns so the strong corner can play tougher on his wide receiver (Diagram 7:6).

C. We double-key the running backs.

    1. On the strong side we key any back going to the strong side with the strong end and strong backer. If the back takes an

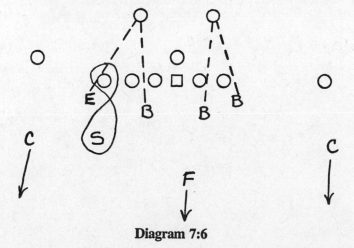

Diagram 7:6

outside route, swing or flat route, the end will take him man-for-man (Diagram 7:7).

2. If the back turns up into the middle on a circle or divided route, the strong backer takes him man-for-man (Diagram 7:8).

3. On the weak side we key any back going to the weak side with the outside backer and the weak side backer. They have the same reads as the strong side. If the back runs an outside pattern, swing or flat route, the outside backer will take him man-for-man (Diagram 7:9).

4. If the back turns inside on a circle or a divide, the weak backer takes him man-for-man (Diagram 7:10).

5. If a back doesn't come to the backers' or ends' area, they carry out their normal Cover 3 zone assignment (Diagram 7:11).

6. If both backs come to the same side, the defender assigned to the first back is determined by the first back's pattern. The backer who did not pick up the first back out starts to his zone area looking for a second back. If the second back shows to his side, the remaining backer will pick him up man-for-man (Diagrams 7:12 and 7:13).

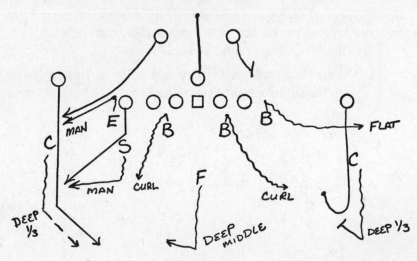

Diagram 7:7

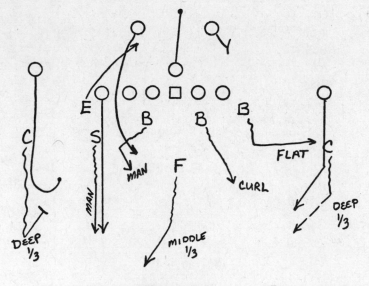

Diagram 7:8

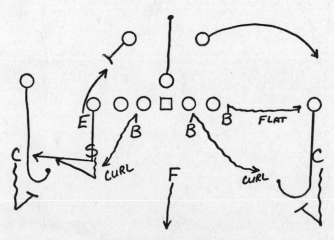

Diagram 7:9

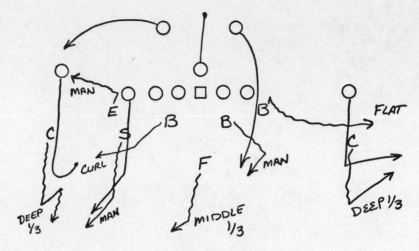

Diagram 7:10

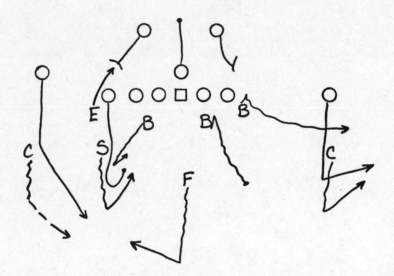

Diagram 7:11

Cover 3 man allows us double covers which are very hard for a quarterback to read because we don't know where they will be until the receivers commit to patterns. It also gives us a way to shut off the tight end or slot back.

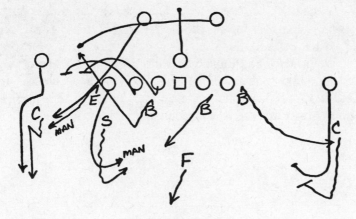

Diagram 7:12

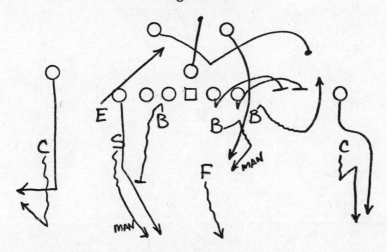

Diagram 7:13

Cover 3 Switch

A. Cover 3 Switch is a three-deep umbrella zone as well. All reads and keys in Cover 3 Switch are the same as in regular Cover 3 except strong-side option.

B. This cover is used as a defensive stunt to demolish the strong-side option.

    C. If the play goes to the weak side or it is a pass or any other type of a run other than an option, the secondary plays a regular 3 cover.

    D. If the offense runs the strong-side option as expected (otherwise we would not be in this cover), the strong safety and strong end change option assignments immediately. The strong end crosses into the backfield and attacks the pitch man. At the same time, the strong safety steps up to attack the quarterback (Diagrams 7:14 and 7:15).

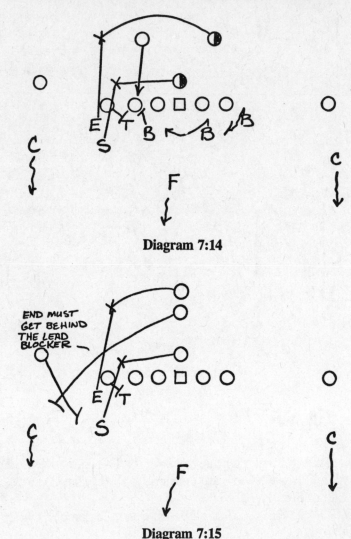

Diagram 7:14

Diagram 7:15

Cover 3 Sting

A. Cover 3 Sting is a three-deep umbrella zone with holdup men on all three quick receivers (Diagram 7:16).

B. We use this cover on long yardage situations. It allows us to slow the receivers down in order to get a better pass rush and to cut down the distance the receivers can travel.

C. The strong safety plays the strong flat, while the outside backer plays the weak flat. However, they align themselves head up on the wide receiver to their side. They must make contact with the receivers and play hard their first move inside or out. From that point they play regular three cover (Diagram 7:17).

D. The strong end must jam the tight end hard before he returns to his regular Cover 3 pass rush.

E. All others play regular Cover 3 techniques and reads.

F. This defense is weak against the weak side draw if the backers don't read well. It was not designed for a third and eight. It's a third and 20 or more defense.

G. If the tight end gets off clean, he can destroy you in this defense. You must jam him hard.

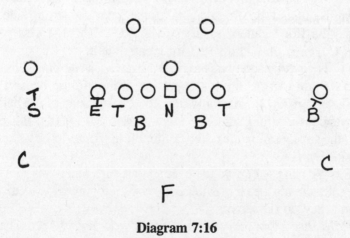

Diagram 7:16

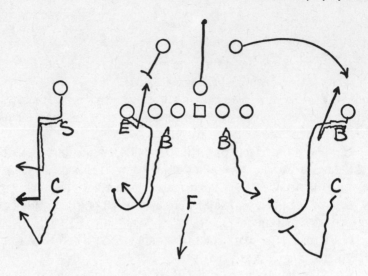

Diagram 7:17

Cover 3 Blood

A. Cover 3 Blood is our garbage defense. It's used against any surprise offensive set.

B. In Cover 3 Blood we drop eight and rush only three.

C. We play a regular Cover 3. Only the strong safety covers the 14 to 20 yards out and the strong end takes the flat to the strong side. This prevents the flood pattern to the strong side. Everyone else plays a regular Cover 3, only at a five-yard greater depth.

D. The strong safety has to read the receiver combinations on his side so we don't waste him to the outside, if the offense doesn't try to flood (Diagram 7:18). He should look for Z at the snap of the ball. If Z goes outside, the strong safety must go outside at 15 yards. If Z comes inside, the strong safety must knock him off his route and try to help to the inside.

E. We can use our blood cover against trips and twins sets. If the strong safety reads the trips patterns by covering moves, you can cover anything they do (Diagrams 7:19-7:21).

F. We use blood cover for twins as well as trip sets. The only changes are the outside backer lines up on the extra weak side receiver and the strong safety moves up on Z (Diagram 7:22).

G. The blood cover is used as a checkoff for any uncertain situations. If a linebacker or one of the safeties makes a blood call, the defense is automatically changed to blood defense. Any other call is off.

H. We use this call against back motion into trips or twins, unless we are in a blitz. These situations will be discussed in a later chapter. It is important, however, to have a defense to handle problem situations.

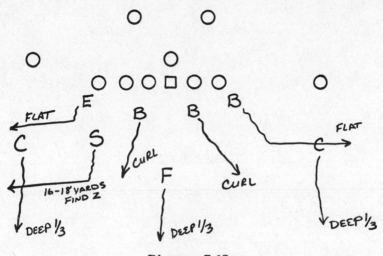

Diagram 7:18

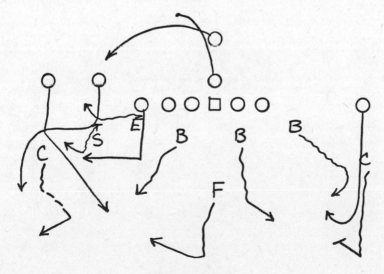

Diagram 7:19

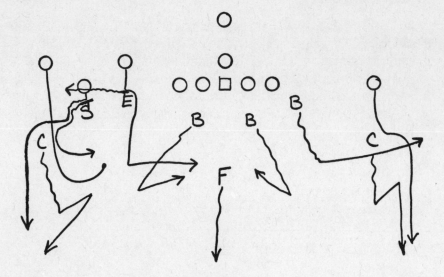

Diagram 7:20

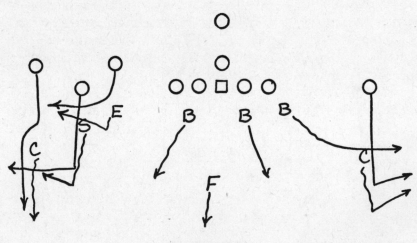

Diagram 7:21

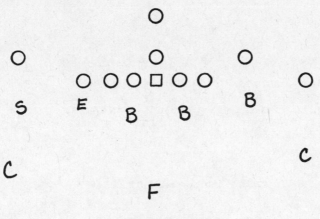

Diagram 7:22

Cover 3 Cheat

A. Cover 3 Cheat is another adjustment we have from our regular Cover 3. We use the Cover 3 Cheat when we are going to blitz with one of the safeties.

B. We will talk about the safety blitz later in Chapter 9. Right now we are concerned with how we cover the receivers when we are sending one of the safeties.

C. When we send the strong safety, we cheat our secondary over to special positions on the field. We have our corners cheat to a yard and a half inside the wide receivers. We are still playing a zone Cover 3, but in this blitz, we are rushing eight men, so that leaves only the three-deep umbrella to cover the quick receivers.

D. We cheat the free safety over to a position of seven yards off the ball and directly in front of the tight end. The strong safety's position is for our weak sellout (Diagram 7:23). On sellouts, the safety always lines up opposite our call.

E. The safety is placed here to prevent the quick pass to the tight end, if the quarterback reads the blitz.

F. The corners are placed inside to stop the quick slant that is used by many teams as a checkoff when a blitz is read.

G. The free safety and the corners read for a quick pass for the first five steps and then break to their regular position (Diagram 7:24).

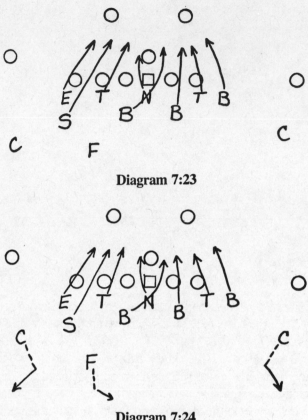

Diagram 7:23

Diagram 7:24

Cover 5

    A. Cover 5 is a change-up defense off Cover 1. It only changes the strong end, outside backer and weak side backer.

    B. The secondary plays a regular Cover 1. All reads and keys are the same.

    C. The difference in Cover 5 and Cover 1 is that our strong end and outside backer crash hard to the football (Diagram 7:25).

    D. With the outside backer crashing, our weak side flat is open. We never want to leave the deep zones or our flat areas open. To prevent having the weak flat open, we have our weak backer go to the weak side flat when he reads pass in Cover 5.

E. By sending him to the weak side flat, we give up the weak side curl area (Diagram 7:26). We would rather have the ball caught in the middle curl area than in the outside perimeter area.

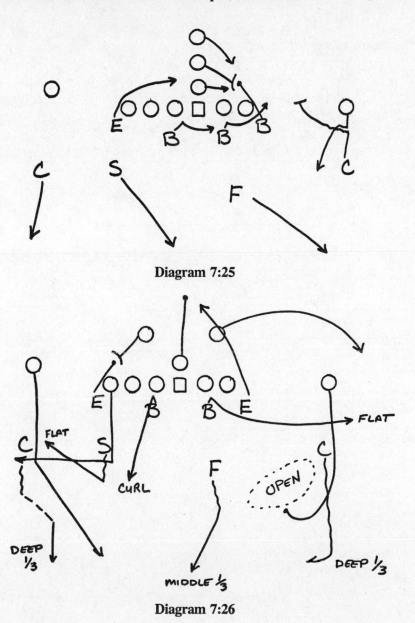

Diagram 7:25

Diagram 7:26

Cover 8

A. Cover 8 is a predetermined roll of our secondary to the weak side.

B. The corner is to attack the weak side receiver X and knock his timing off on any route he is to run.

C. When we are predetermining our secondary roll, we will normally slant our defense away from where the secondary is rolling.

D. In Cover 8 we do not read backs for our roll. We are going to roll on X no matter what the backs do.

E. Cover 8 gives us an opportunity on a key down to roll up and knock the offense's favorite receiver off his route (Diagram 7:27).

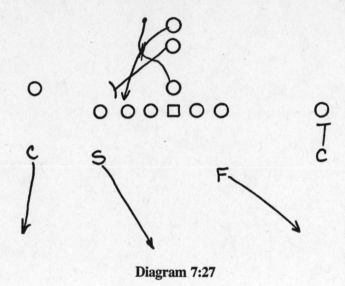

Diagram 7:27

Cover 9

A. Cover 9 is a predetermined roll of our secondary to the strong side.

B. The corner is to attack the strong side receiver Z and knock his timing off on any route he is to run.

C. We use this cover against a slot too.

    1. Against a slot, we have to determine which receiver we want to hit, X or Z.

    2. If we are to hit Z, the strong safety will roll up.

    3. If we are to hit X in the slot set, we will roll up the strong corner.

D. In Cover 9 we do not read backs for our roll. We are going to roll on Z no matter what the backs do.

E. Cover 9 gives us the same opportunity that Cover 8 gives us, only Cover 9 lets us strike either receiver on the strong side (Diagram 7:28). We predetermine by scouting which receiver it will be.

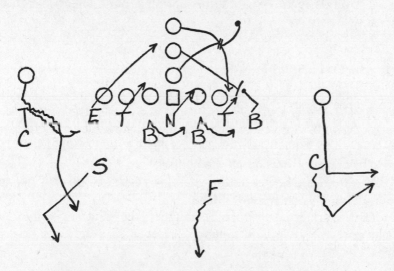

Diagram 7:28. Cover 9 roll Z against a pro set.

The only other cover we run is one we use against a team which has only one outstanding receiver whom they may try to hide by moving him from X to Z. They may also put him in motion or in a slot.

To counter these offensive adjustments we use our special roll call. In this cover we call the number of the receiver we want to roll to. *Example:* If their best receiver is number *88*, our huddle call would be roll *88*. When the offense breaks from the huddle and we identify the formation and where number *88* is lined up, the free safety will make an eight or nine cover call. If number *88* is in slot, Cover 3 will be called and the strong safety will be the attacker.

8

COVERS 4, 6, AND 7

In this chapter we will talk about man cover, other than goal line, and our special cover designed for slot teams as well as our 5-under cover used against twin sets.

Cover 4

A. Cover 4 is a straight man-for-man defense. The corners play man on the wide receivers or tight end in slot or double-tight offenses. The strong safety plays man-for-man on the tight end or slot back. The free safety is man-for-man on the halfback.

B. We use Cover 4 on the goal line against twins or trips, and against motion when we are blitzing.

C. We prefer to stay out of a straight Cover 4 if at all possible. We would rather play Cover 4 combo. In Cover 4 we have no help or double-cover possibilities.

Cover 4 Combo

A. In Cover 4 Combo we play the strong safety man-for-man on the tight end or slot back. The corners are man-for-man on the wide receivers or tight end against a slot.

B. The free safety is free to play the ball or help where he sees help is needed.

C. The linebackers play the same as they did in Cover 3 man. They will double-key the backs for inside or outside patterns.

D. The linebackers who do not draw a back assignment will go to their zones, or in the case of the strong end, will rush the quarterback. These drops are shown in Diagram 8:1.

    E. We have a rule we use in our man covers that I feel is very important. It's called our *eight-yard rule*. It's used mostly against slot sets but it can be used any time two receivers line up within eight yards of each other. Our call is *inside-out*. We have shortened this call to *inside*. This means that even though we are playing man-for-man, we will switch on any crossing patterns run by the two close receivers. In the case of a crossing pattern, the two defensive backs (usually the strong safety and strong corner) jump on the receiver's first move and then look to the other receiver. If the other receiver's pattern will bring him across the defensive back's face, he releases his receiver to take the new receiver man-for-man (Diagrams 8:2-8:5).

    F. We use this a lot on the goal line.

    G. We use the inside call against the goal line pick. The defensive back, whose man picks, must immediately switch to the receiver who is free (Diagram 8:6).

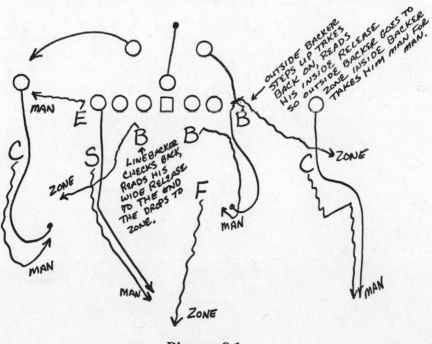

Diagram 8:1

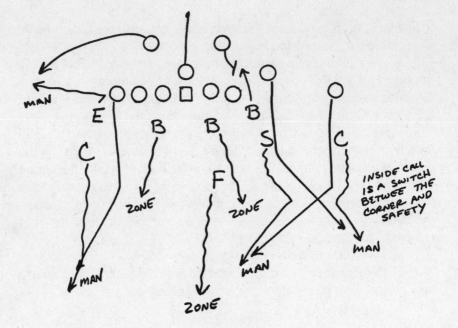

Diagram 8:2

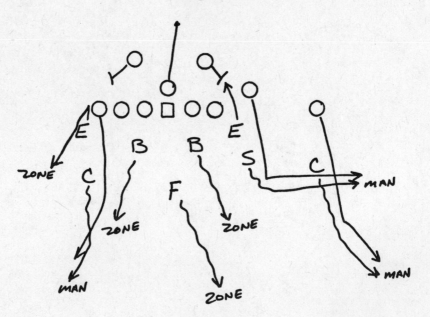

Diagram 8:3

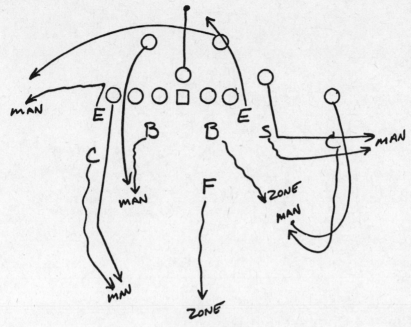

Diagram 8:4

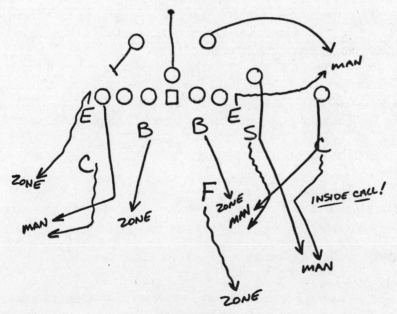

Diagram 8:5

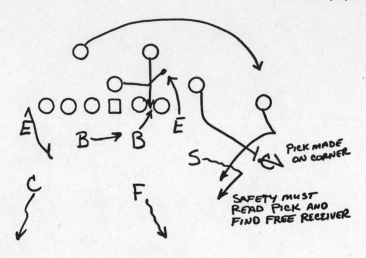

Diagram 8:6

Cover 4 Combo (Tight)

This cover is used to stop a delay-passing game or screen attack.

A. In the regular Cover 4 Combo, if a back doesn't move into a pattern, the undercover goes to their zones.

B. In Cover 4 Combo (tight) the inside linebackers will not drop to zone if the backs set up to block. They will wait three yards off the ball for a possible delay or screen to the back out.

C. The strong safety and both corners are still playing man all the way.

D. The free safety is still zoning in the middle to help on any deep pass.

E. The outside backer and strong end will both rush hard. Diagram 8:7 shows our *Cover 4 Combo Tight, Four Tight.*

Cover 6 Slot Combo

A. Cover 6 is a cover designed to cover a slot-passing attack.

B. It is a combination defense. Half of the defense is playing a zone and the other half is playing man.

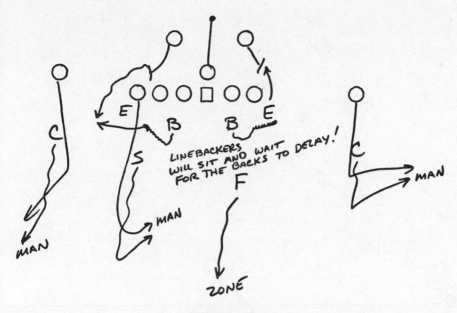

Diagram 8:7

C. The zone side of the defense is on the slot side.

D. The tight end side of the formation is played man-for-man.

E. The strong safety lines up over the slot at seven yards. He reads the same as Cover 1. The only difference is that if strong action shows, he has the deep outside third. If weak action shows, he will cover the middle.

F. The strong corner reads the same as Cover 1. If strong action shows, he will force the wide receiver inside and play his first move tough until someone crosses his face to the outside (Diagram 8:8). His responsibility is the flat. If he reads weak action, he will play regular Cover 1 and cover his deep outside (Diagram 8:9).

G. The free safety reads the same as Cover 1. If he reads strong action, he must close to the slot side and pick up any inside move by either receiver (Diagram 8:8). If he reads weak action, he will play regular Cover 1 (Diagram 8:9).

H. Weak linebacker will read the same as Cover 1. If strong action is read, the weak backer drives hard to the curl, looking for any inside short move (Diagram 8:9).

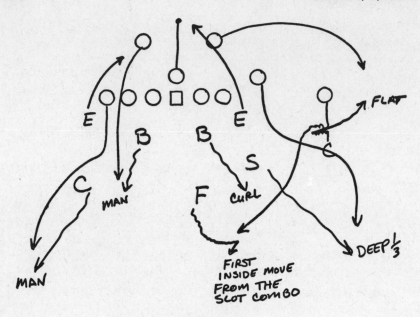

Diagram 8:8

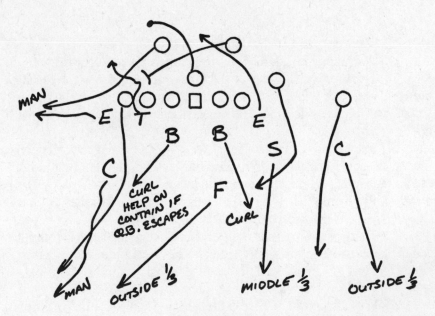

Diagram 8:9

I. The weak side corner plays the tight end man-for-man weak or strong action.

    1. If the tight end blocks down, he comes up to help on the run.
    2. If the tight end releases, the weak corner goes all the way with him.

J. The strong end and the strong backer have their double key as in Cover 4 for any back coming to their side.

K. If the outside backer reads strong action, he rushes. If he reads weak, he plays Cover 1 (Diagram 8:8).

L. It is highly unlikely that a team running slot combinations will run both receivers inside. With the tight end side playing man, we can release our free safety to attack any inside pattern (Diagram 8:10).

The strong end will rush if the back doesn't run a pattern; the free safety can attack the curl and disregard the tight end's post because of the back side man cover. Weak side run action reads Cover 1 to the strong side. Weak side plays are man reads (Diagram 8:11).

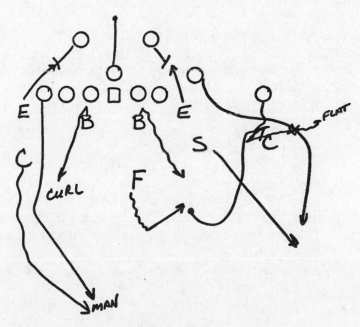

Diagram 8:10

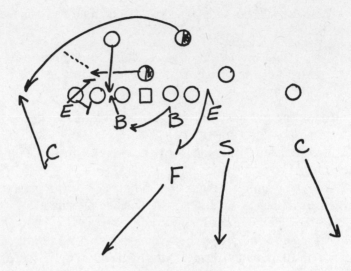

Diagram 8:11

Cover 7 Zone

A. Cover 7 is our answer to the popular five-under, two-deep secondary.

B. We keep our safeties in the deep zones. Each safety has to cover half the field. This can be accomplished with success if the safeties are taught the proper way to play their halves of the field.

    1. At the snap of the ball, both safeties must quickly get to the middle of their half of the field.

    2. They must continue to gain ground as long as any receiver is challenging them deep.

    3. If there is only one receiver deep in their zone, they can cheat over to him, always reading the quarterback (Diagram 8:12).

    4. If there are two receivers deep in a zone, the safety must stay between them.

    5. The safety must take advantage of quarterback keys as to where the ball is going.

       a. *Shoulders*—Safety must open his hips to the side to which the quarterback's shoulders are open. The key to a two-deep is that the safety opens his hips but does not

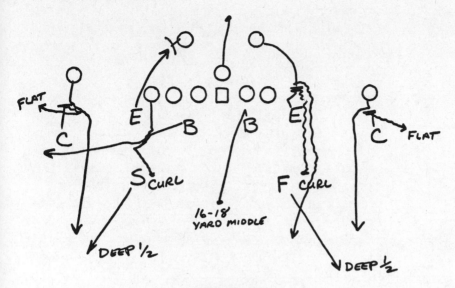

Diagram 8:12

move to either side. He will continue to retreat with his hips open to the quarterback's shoulders. If the quarterback rolls his shoulders around to the other half of the field, the safety rolls his hips to open to that side. He may now begin to cheat to this side. He can cheat now because the receiver is deeper and the quarterback is running out of time and must throw deeper.

b. *Lead Hand on the Ball*—The safety stays in the middle until the quarterback takes his lead hand off the ball. At this time the safety will break to the side where the quarterback is looking.

c. *Quarterback's Chin*—It is important for the secondary to read the quarterback's face. Not just at his eyes for direction, but at his chin. To get the proper arch on a deep pass, the quarterback must tilt his head back. If the chin is up, the quarterback is going to throw deep. If the quarterback is going to drill the ball on a short pass, his chin will be down so he can fire the ball.

d. *The Quarterback's Lead Arm*—If the quarterback's lead arm comes up over his face, he is going to throw deep. If the quarterback's lead arm stays low, he is going to throw short. These are key things to have your defensive backs learn to read. It can give them a good jump on the ball. Remember, the closer the receiver is to the quarterback, the closer the defensive back must be to the receiver.

6. Both corners, at the snap of the ball, play our short zone or weak side technique. They both attack the wide receivers and force them to the inside. The corners will jump on the wide receivers' first move and play them tough until someone crosses their face going to the outside (Diagram 8:13).

7. The strong end must jam the tight end to keep him out of a deep pattern. The strong end will go with the tight end to about the 12-yard strong curl. At this point he will zone.

8. The strong side back looks to knock the tight end off any crossing route and then go to his deep 18-yard middle drop (Diagram 8:13).

9. The outside backer will assume the strong end's pass rush because the strong end is now in pass cover. If a back shows, he must knock him off a deep route (Diagram 8:13).

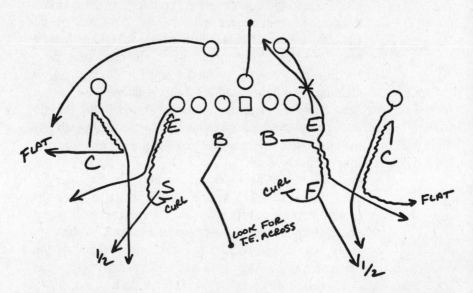

Diagram 8:13

10. The weak side backer must drop straight back to the weak side curl area and read for back out. If a back shows in the seam, he must knock him off a deep route and then go to his curl (Diagram 8:14).

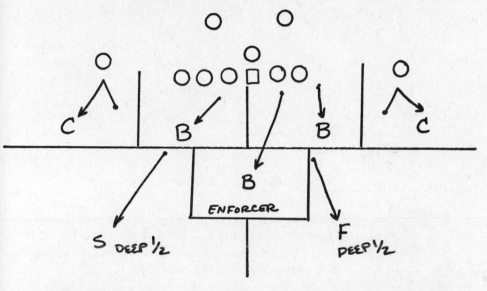

Diagram 8:14. Cover 7—Shows defensive zones without receivers.

Cover 7 zone is good against any set that has only two wide receivers; however, if an offense goes to three or four wide receivers, Cover 7 zone will not work. It would be too easy for the offense to get three receivers deep to split our deep cover. In this case we check off to Cover 7 Man.

Cover 7 Man

In Cover 7 Man we run a five under man-for-man and a two-deep zone behind. Cover 7 Man looks like the zone cover only both our ends are in man cover (Diagram 8:15).

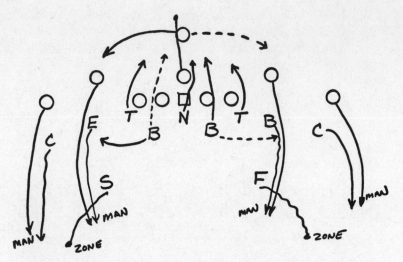

Diagram 8:15. Cover 7 man vs. twins (2 receivers to each side).

Tackles must keep outside contained. Both of our inside backers read the remaining back. The backer on the side he goes to has his man. The other backer is in the pass rush (Diagram 8:16).

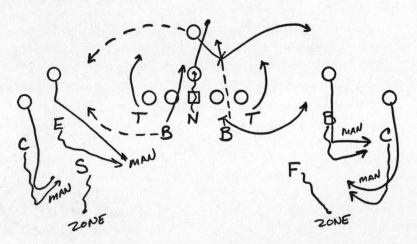

Diagram 8:16. Cover 7 man vs. four wide outs.

Diagrams 8:17 and 8:18 show Cover 7 vs. the strong side option and weak side option:

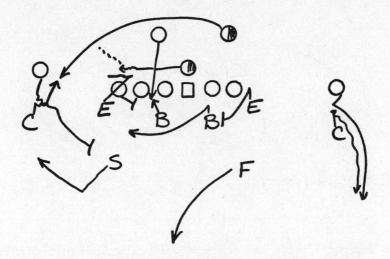

Diagram 8:17

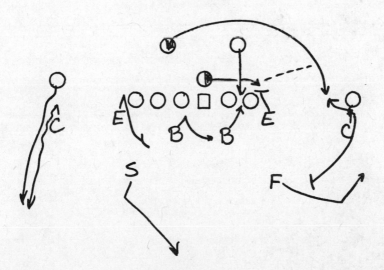

Diagram 8:18

Diagram 8:19 shows enforcer getting into one possible inside pattern. The enforcer becomes very important because offenses will try to hit the no-man's land between safeties and linebackers. The diagram also shows defensive adjustment to splits.

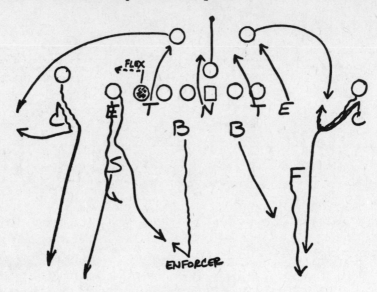

Diagram 8:19

9

BLITZES, BINGOS AND SELLOUTS

All of our blitzes are especially designed to free a specific rusher at a specific place. It is important that all blitzes be designed to use the available personnel to their maximum. Many coaches use the blitz only to surprise the offense from time to time. When it is used only as an occasional surprise, most defenses depend on the surprise to break someone free. Many teams will only send one linebacker when they are trying to sneak someone through. If the linebacker is picked up, this leaves the quarterback with an easy read as to which zone to throw the ball. A blitz of any kind must be designed to attack a certain offensive weakness or to outnumber available offensive blockers. A blitz that is blocked by the offense puts three times the normal pressure on the secondary without undercover help.

Our whole defensive unit is involved in any of our blitzes. The secondary has the job of preventing any quick dump pass that would be used to beat the blitz. The second job of our secondary is to cover receivers close enough to pick off any hurried or poor passes.

It is necessary in any blitz that the blitzing backers camouflage their intent and still be able to execute their assigned task with speed and agility, but with control. Control is important so that the linebacker can read as he attacks. If he reads run, he must try to get into the play. If he reads pass, he must try to get pressure on the quarterback as quickly as possible. A blitzing backer can never pass up a back in his lane. This is the most important point. Our ends will never run past a back nor will our linebackers. In this way we don't have backs slipping out into screens or into delay patterns.

Our blitzes and bingos are designed to get the quarterback quickly. Most important is to prevent the quarterback from setting up. The other important factor for a team that is going to blitz is to prepare for a quarterback who can read the blitz and get rid of the ball quickly. The secondary must be alert and prepared to prevent a quick pass to the tight end or wide receiver to beat the blitz.

An important coaching point in any blitz is to teach the linebackers as well as the linemen to tackle any and all backs in their lanes. If the back is a receiver, this prevents his pattern and if he has the ball, he must be tackled. Tackling backs in the pass rush lanes prevents screens and delay patterns from beating the blitz.

We have several blitzes we use to attack the different offenses. The first blitz is our *Eagle Blitz* (Diagram 9:1).

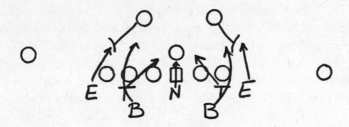

Diagram 9:1

In the Eagle Blitz we are usually looking for a sprint-out or rollout passing attack. It is very effective against power off tackle and speed option offenses. The strong end and outside backer drive hard at the quarterback. If the back comes at them, they are to make contact and stay with him. This occupies him so he cannot help to block the linebackers. The end and outside backer must not allow the back to release into a pattern. The tackles are to close down across the offensive tackle's face and attack the offensive guard. This is designed to draw the offensive tackle inside on our tackle and still have our tackle tie up the offensive guards. The backers drive hard and low to the outside, reading as they go. The noseman must control the center and read for draw.

Blitzes are imperative for a good secondary. Pass rush is what makes good secondaries. Pass rush makes for rushed passes, mistimed patterns, poor, blocked and tipped passes.

The *Stack Blitz* is a blitz we use a lot against teams which like to use a lot of play-action passes. We use the stack because it is very tough against the run (Diagram 9:2).

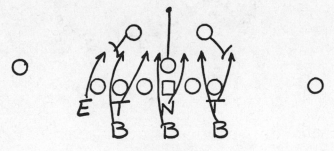

Diagram 9:2

In the Stack Blitz we slant the down linemen one way and send the backers the other. In Diagram 9:2 we have slanted the linemen weak. This is not something we like to do because our weak tackle has to attack the weak back. His job now becomes that of the weak backer. He cannot allow the back to escape into a pattern. The down linemen slant across the offensive linemen's face to attack the next offensive lineman and tie him up. The backers attack hard and low, reading as they move. Any play action is attacked in this same way. We would prefer to run the Stack Blitz with the slant to the strong side (Diagram 9:3).

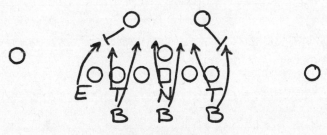

Diagram 9:3

When we slant to the strong or weak side, we don't slant the strong end. It also keeps all our assignments the same because now we have the outbacker taking on the weak back.

The *Forty Defense* is our even defense. Our forty blitz is very much like our strong slant stack blitz. We slant our weak side down linemen inside to close it off. The strong tackle penetrates the gap while the strong and weak backers attack the first outside gap (Diagram 9:4).

We can adjust outside pressure to our pass rush just by calling Cover 5. In Cover 5 our strong end and outside backer crash to the ball.

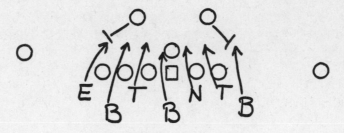

Diagram 9:4

In this cover they have no back reads or responsibility for the flat. They are free to crash hard to the football. This can be very effective against outside veer teams (Diagram 9:5).

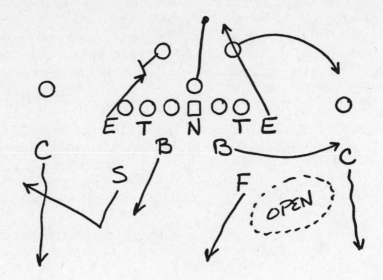

Diagram 9:5

This is one of our most effective blitzes because when the offensive linemen read our backers dropping off, they tend to relax and look to help too late on the outside. This defense is deceptive because the quarterback believes the weak flat is open. It is not an easy job for the weak backer, but our backers have always covered well.

Our *Bingos* are blitzes run right up the pipe. We never determine in the huddle which way our bingos will go. We wait until we see the offensive formation to determine the direction of the bingo. There are four things that will determine which way we will bingo. These are:

1. Scouting;
2. Formation;
3. Field position (wide or short side);
4. Down and distance to go.

For most situations the formation and field position will determine which way we will send the backers. Diagram 9:6 shows our weak bingo.

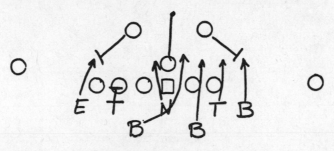

Diagram 9:6

You notice the noseman always goes opposite on the bingos. The strong tackle has no help, so he must play head up and control both gaps on either side of the offensive tackle. The noseman must take the center's head as he goes. The strong and weak backers both blow by either side of the weak guard. The end and outside backer come hard to contact the backs.

If the backs disappear into the line, the end and outside backer drive hard to the quarterback. If the backs come to them, they must control the backs and not let them escape.

The strong side bingo is much the same only in the other direction (Diagram 9:7).

The noseman again goes opposite. The weak tackle must now play head up and play both sides of the offensive tackle. Both inside backers blow by the strong side offensive guard.

Our *fifty-two tight blitz* is one we like to use on short yardage situations. The fifty-two tight gives our defense a split-six look out of our okie defense. In a short yardage situation our tight blitz puts a lot of pressure on any attempt at a play-action pass (Diagram 9:8).

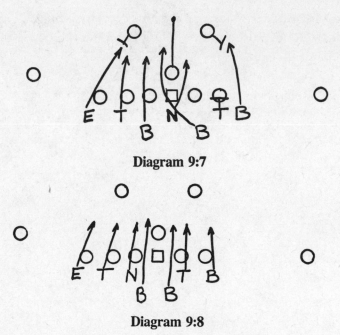

Diagram 9:7

Diagram 9:8

The tight defense demands that we play a Cover 8. Cover 8 gives us the weak side run support needed to make this an effective short-yardage defense (Diagram 9:9).

Strong safety must look for a quick pass to the tight end while the strong corner must look for play-action slant to the Z receiver.

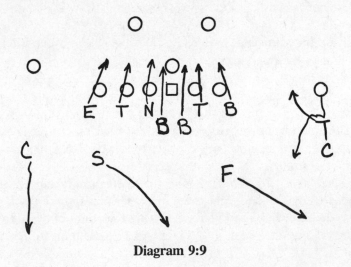

Diagram 9:9

Our strongest blitz involves our strong safety. When we send a safety, we call it a *Sellout*. When we sellout, we are sending eight people. We must reach the quarterback quickly. He cannot be allowed to set up. If he can avoid the pressure, our secondary is in big trouble. Hence, the name sellout. Our sellouts are run off our bingos only when we add one of our safeties to make it an eight-man rush. Diagram 9:10 shows our basic strong sellout.

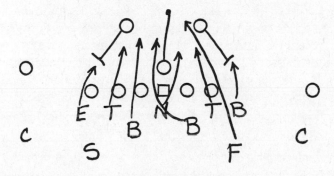

Diagram 9:10

In our sellouts we use a special three cover. Our corners play inside shade to protect against a quick slant. The strong safety lines up over the inside shoulder of the tight end at seven yards. His job is to prevent a quick pass to the tight end. After the threat of a quick pass is gone, the strong safety and corners play a regular three-deep cover.

The only difference between the strong bingo and strong sellout, other than that the safety is going, is that the weak side tackle does not have to play head up—he can attack the inside gap.

In our weak sellout we have the strong safety and free safety on the same side of the field. This is an easy read for a quarterback, so we align as normally as possible and then walk into the positions shown in the drawings. We try to time the snap so we get our free safety in position at the snap to cover the tight end. Diagram 9:11 shows the weak sellout.

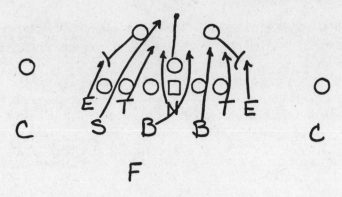

Diagram 9:11

The corners and free safety must protect against the quick pass. Our blitzes are a very necessary part of our secondary covers. The pressure created by these defensive tactics accounts for many key plays all season long. The pass rush is what makes a good secondary great. If a quarterback can't stand and read a secondary, he must throw blindly into the coverage. This is what a good pass rush does. It can cause deflected, poor, or floated passes, any of which can be an interception or a receiver's epitaph.

10

MOTION ADJUSTMENTS AND SPECIAL SITUATIONS

In this section on motion and special situations we will discuss changing covers due to formations, shifts or motion. It is possible to call a cover in the huddle that is not the cover you want to be in when the offense comes to the line of scrimmage. You must be able to adjust. You could be in a certain cover and the offense shifts into a different formation. You will want to change your cover. It is becoming more and more common to be in a certain cover and the offense will send someone in motion which can change the cover you are in. It is possible to have all of these changes occur prior to the snap of the ball. This means that the secondary must be prepared to handle any and all of these changes.

In order to handle motion it is important that the coach teach the types of motion and the reasons for the motion.

There are basically five types of motion. They are:

1. Slot motion to wing or flanker (Diagram 10:1).
2. Flanker or wing motion to slot (Diagram 10:2).
3. Back motion to trips (Diagram 10:3).
4. Back motion to twins (Diagram 10:4).
5. Tight end shifts and fullback motions.

There are many types or ways to change formations by motion, but for the most part, the first four listed are the most common.

This type of motion (motion 1) is used either to bring the slot back into a running back position to be used as a blocker or third back or for deception to observe secondary adjustments.

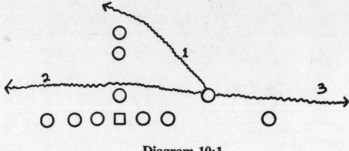

Diagram 10:1

This type of motion (motion 2) is used to change the formation strength, hide a receiver the offense doesn't want bumped or to bring a blocker over to help on a certain play.

This motion (motion 3) is used to open wide gaps in zone defenses to make it easier for the quarterback to find a seam.

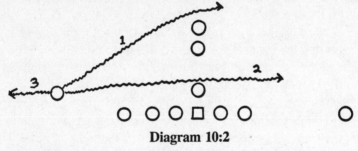

Diagram 10:2

This type of motion (motion 1) is used to bring the flanker back into a running back position.

The number 2 type of motion is used to change the formation strength or to put both wide receivers on the same side of the field. It is also a way to bring a moving blocker over to the other side of the formation.

The number 3 motion is used to widen the seams in the defense by spreading out the secondary.

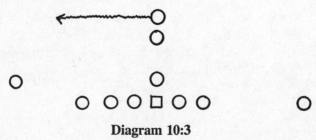

Diagram 10:3

This type of motion is used to put three quick receivers on one side. It also puts two potential blockers far outside on the perimeter. Although a trips set is primarily a passing set it can be used for a very strong sweep.

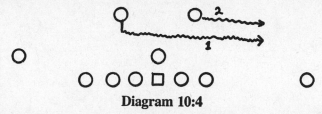

Diagram 10:4

Motion to twins can be difficult to handle because the offense may be disguising a trips set they wish to use on the back side of the formation. Diagrams 10:5 and 10:6 show how twins can be used to hide a trips set.

Motion 1 gives two wide receivers to each side with the remaining back to the motion side.

Motion 2 puts two wide receivers to each side with the remaining back on the side, away from the motion. It makes it difficult to roll a zone when you're not sure which side they're going to. Diagram 10:5— twins motion being used to hide trips set away from the motion.

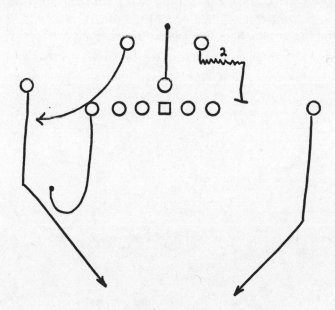

Diagram 10:5

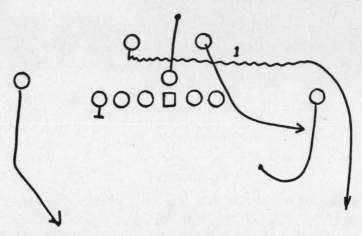

Diagram 10:6

Twins and trips are treated as almost the same formation by our secondary. in trips we will cheat the free safety to the three-receiver side while in twins we want to keep him directly in the middle of the four receivers. Diagrams 10:7B and 10:8B also show back motion that can change twins to trips and trips to twins, if the offense comes out and shifts to a set and then motions out of it. Diagram 10:7A shows the set and Diagram 10:7B shows the offensive set change with motion.

With motion, this set is read as trips. However, if the tight end blocks and the weak back runs a pattern, we again have twins.

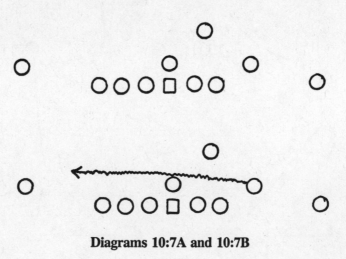

Diagrams 10:7A and 10:7B

Another possible combination is in Diagrams 10:8A and 10:8B. Here the formation from the huddle would be read as trips. However, there is a possible twins set on the back side.

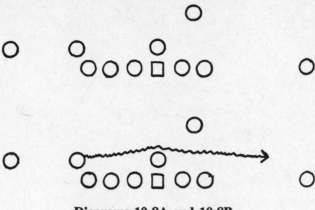

Diagrams 10:8A and 10:8B

This set is also very good for a quick pitch to the weak side. Consider this possibility before you try to solve these secondary problems.

Diagrams 10:9A, 10:9B, 10:9C and 10:9D show offensive set, shift, motion and the pattern run at the snap of the ball. How is your secondary going to handle this?

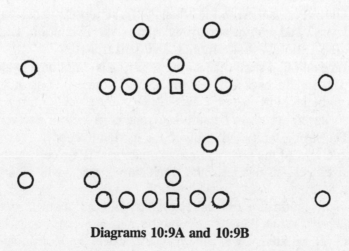

Diagrams 10:9A and 10:9B

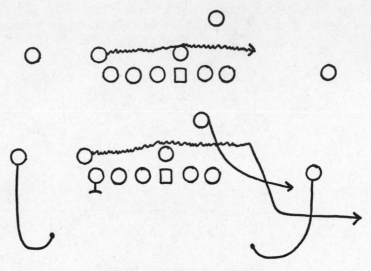

Diagrams 10:9C and 10:9D

How is your secondary going to handle these changes? Could they handle them? If you don't have an easy adjustment to handle these situations, the secondary can easily become confused.

One of the biggest problems with trying to cover trips, twins and motion sets is that the coach will try to teach each set as a special situation and needs a special cover. We feel that special situations must all be treated the same. That is, we should have one cover to handle all these situations.

The slot or flanker motion is handled by simply changing our cover to a Cover 3 and we run our strong safety with the motion. Diagrams 10:10 and 10:11 show slot motion and flanker motion.

When motion starts, the strong safety calls "motion" to alert the secondary and linebackers. He will then call "three." Even though we prefer to be in a three against the slot, the strong safety must still call "three" several times to be sure everyone is in the same cover.

The strong safety will go with the motion man only as far as the next receiver. At the point the motion man passes a receiver, the next defensive back (in this case the weak side corner), will pick up the motion man.

In this motion the first call, again, is "motion" to alert secondary and linebackers that there is going to be a change in cover. No matter what cover we are in, we will change to Cover 3. We can stay in a

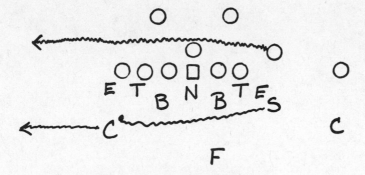

Diagram 10:10. Slot Motion.

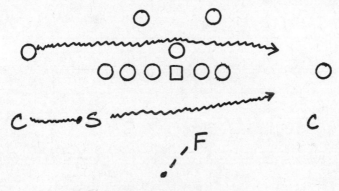

Diagram 10:11. Flanker motion.

4-Combo if our scouting tells us it's a good cover for a slot set. Again, the cover "three" must be called across. We would make a "combo" call if we were blitzing and a slot or flanker motion showed. We would still blitz and we would still run our strong safety. If we only had a "three" call, we would have to call off the blitz because we would have no flat cover. To blitz with no flat cover is too high a risk for us to take.

We can handle trips or twins or any special set with our "three blood." In blood we drop eight men and rush only three. Diagram 10:12 shows the zones of responsibility for three blood.

The strong safety must read in the 14- to 18-yard zone for the out first and the curl or short post second. The strong safety is on the three-receiver side to prevent an overload or flood pattern (Diagram 10:13).

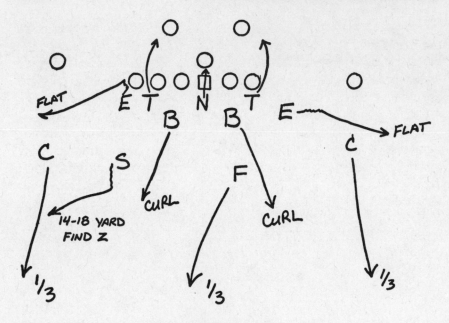

Diagram 10:12

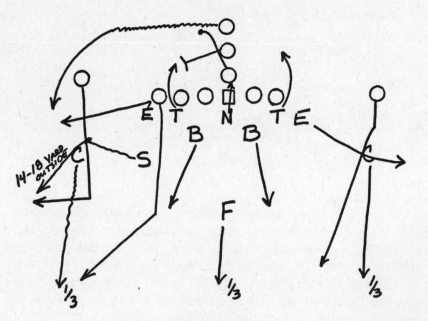

Diagram 10:13

Any trips or twins set or motion into either trips or twins makes our immediate call "blood." A "blood" call changes any defense to blood. The only time twins and trips will not put us into a blood cover is when we are blitzing. When we are blitzing, we do not want to change out of our blitz so we can't run a *blood cover*. For most blitzes we are in a 4-Combo Cover. This puts us in a man-for-man cover with a free safety.

If the offense comes out in trips or twins or motions into trips or twins, we have to change our cover from 4-Combo to four straight. This means that the free safety must pick up the fourth receiver. Diagrams 10:14, 10:15, 10:16 and 10:17 show different situations which can cause us to change covers but will not take us out of our blitz.

When two receivers get within eight yards of each other, our call is *inside*. This means that the safety will take the first receiver who comes inside, the corner will take the first outside receiver.

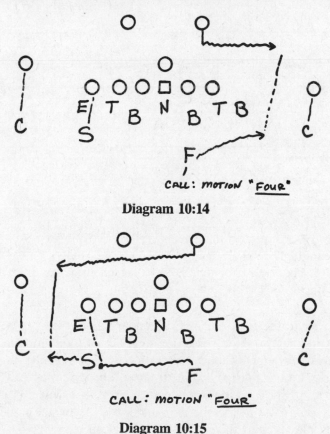

CALL: MOTION "FOUR"

Diagram 10:14

CALL: MOTION "FOUR"

Diagram 10:15

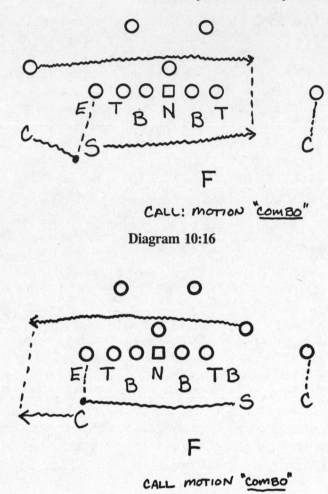

CALL: MOTION "COMBO"

Diagram 10:16

CALL MOTION "COMBO"

Diagram 10:17. With slot motion there is no fourth receiver so we can stay in combo and keep our free safety. The motion does not affect the blitzes in any of these situations.

To stay in the blitz call, the secondary must pick up the extra receiver with the free safety. The free safety moves with motion to the next receiver. A defensive back never crosses over a receiver; the free safety picks up the tight end; the strong safety now moves with the motion man. In this situation, we would check off to a Cover 3 vs. trips. The strong safety would play the short under zone, while the corners and free safety play 3-deep zones. The blitz stays on.

With flanker motion there is no fourth receiver so we move the strong safety with motion, but we keep a free safety and a man cover on the three receivers (Diagram 10:17).

The greatest adjustment our defense as a whole, and our secondary as a unit, have to make is when we are in a sellout and motion shows. Motion from the slot or flanker is not as great a problem as back motion to trips or twins. When we are in sellout and motion shows, we still want to stay in the blitz. We can't stay in our special three against back motion because there are now four receivers and our end and outside backer are committed to the blitz, so they can't help. With a back becoming a fourth receiver, we have to get out of the sellout because we need the safety to help in the cover of the fourth receiver. However, with the offense pulling a back out of a blocking position, this means there is still a great advantage to a seven-man blitz. We will make a motion call, change our blitz from sellout (which is an eight-man blitz) to bingo (which is a seven-man blitz) and change our cover to a four straight vs. twins and a three vs. trips. If the motion is a flanker or a slot, we will go to strong sellout and send our free safety. Our rule is, if motion starts or ends in slot, we go to strong sellout (Diagram 10:18A).

Diagrams 10:18B and 10:18C show the defense set for weak sellout, cover cheat three. Motion shows and calls are shown with adjustments. Diagram 10:18C shows the blitz vs. the sellout change.

The calls are shown next to the positions that should make the calls. The numbers indicate the sequence in which the calls should be made. The lemon call informs the front seven which direction the bingo will be run.

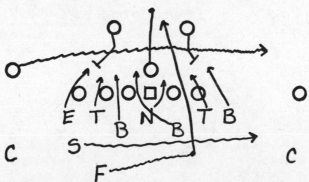

Diagram 10:18A. Huddle call was weak sellout: Motion to the slot makes our call strong sellout.

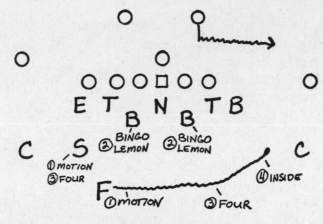

Diagram 10:18B

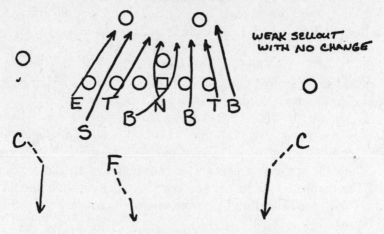

Diagram 10:18C

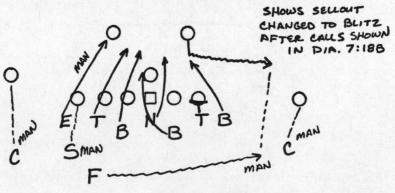

Diagram 10:18D

The defense changes to bingo lemon and now will blitz to the remaining backs' side to protect against the run. The weak side tackle must play head-up and control both gaps. The strong safety does not go; he must now play cover four man-to-man on the tight end. With the motion, we must pick up the fourth receiver with the free safety. This means we can't send the strong safety because he has to pick up the tight end. The linebackers must now change their direction of attack. The weak back has gone in motion, leaving only the strong side running back. We now want our linebackers to attack the remaining back's side. Our linebackers' call now becomes *Bingo*, taking us out of the sellout and *Lemon* meaning we are going to the left side where the remaining back is. We attack the remaining back's side to prevent any attempt to run the ball. In the next few drawings we will show other situations that can either take us out of a sellout or just change our cover so we can stay in our sellout (Diagrams 10:19 through 10:21).

With these situations as examples, it should be easy to understand that complicated situations can be controlled easily with proper preparation by the secondary. We can either drop eight to cover all zones when motion shows, or we can rush seven or eight, depending on the motion. The blitz against trips and twins is very effective. It is important to both cover and attack special sets. The methods we use here against trips and twins are applied to shotguns and outpost offenses as well.

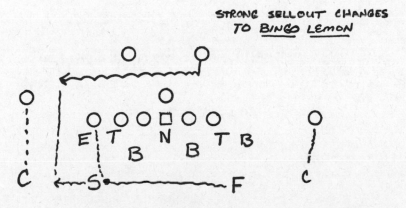

STRONG SELLOUT CHANGES
TO *BINGO LEMON*

CALLS: *MOTION FOUR* , LINEBACKERS CALL: *BINGO LEMON*

Diagram 10:19

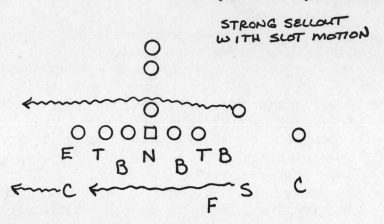

CALLS: MOTION THREE, LINEBACKERS CALLS: NONE
SELLOUT IS STILL ON, THERE ARE STILL ONLY 3 RECEIVERS

Diagram 10:20

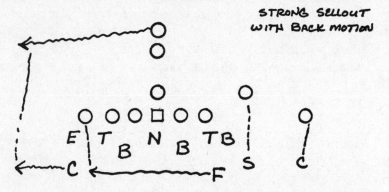

CALLS: MOTION FOUR, LINEBACKERS CALL: BINGO RED
WHEN THE REMAINING BACK IS IN THE MIDDLE WE WILL
BINGO TO THE TWO RECEIVERS OR WIDE SIDE OF THE FIELD.

Diagram 10:21

Tight End Shifts

Many teams will try to confuse defensive assignments by shifting the tight end from one side of the formation to the other. This shift will move the strength of the formation from one side to the other (Diagrams 10:22A and 10:22B).

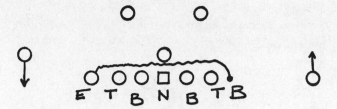

OFFENSE COMES OUT IN TIGHT LEFT AND
THEN SHIFTS TO TIGHT RIGHT.

Diagram 10:22A

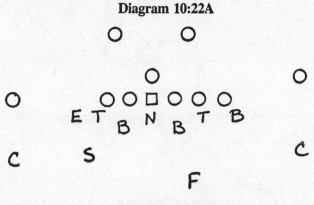

Diagram 10:22B

Tight end shifts can be made quickly and the ball can be snapped before the defense has time to make all of its needed adjustments. This simple offensive move suddenly makes your weak safety strong, your strong safety weak and the strong corner now must make weak reads. In this situation we always flop our safeties over, but never the corners (Diagram 10:23).

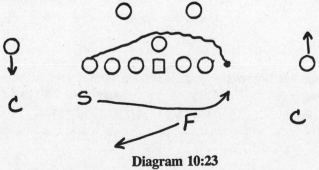

Diagram 10:23

Tight end motions, to be legal, call for the other two receivers to be on the line of scrimmage. In this instance, the tight end is nothing more than a slot back. Tight end motions are shown in Diagrams 10:24A through 10:24C.

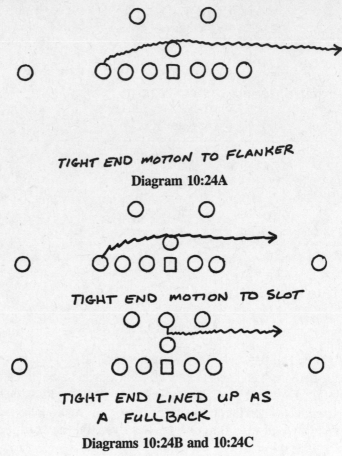

TIGHT END MOTION TO FLANKER

Diagram 10:24A

TIGHT END MOTION TO SLOT

**TIGHT END LINED UP AS
A FULLBACK**

Diagrams 10:24B and 10:24C

Zip-Zap

Another type of motion which is becoming more and more popular is the Zip-Zap motion. Zip is normal motion across the ball to the other side of the formation. Zap is motion which starts across the formation and suddenly turns and goes back the same direction it came. This is shown in Diagram 10:25.

The aim of this type of motion is to cause the defense to adjust to a formation change which is not really going to happen. This can be very perplexing to the defense. If the defense is changed too soon for the apparent formation change, and the motion goes back, a second defensive change may cause confusion or may not allow time to be carried out before the snap. For these reasons our basic adjustment to this type of motion is Cover 3. As shown in Diagram 10:26, our strong safety will mirror the motion man.

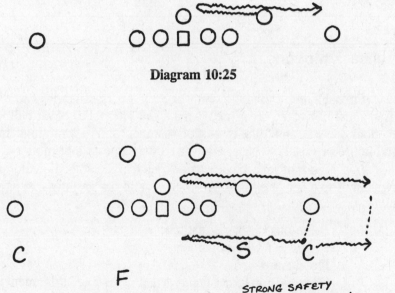

Diagram 10:25

Diagram 10:26

In this situation the strong safety should be placed in the middle and the secondary put into a Cover 3. With the strong safety in the middle, he can go either way with the motion (Diagram 10:27).

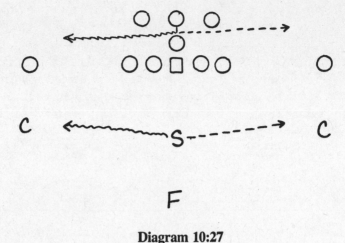

Diagram 10:27

Fullback Motions

Fullback motions are the same as back motions to twins and trips. They must be treated the same. Some teams attempt to cover halfback motions one way and fullback motions another. Fullback motions, from full-house or wishbone sets, are treated the same as slot motions.

It is important for each defensive back to understand that motions, twin and triple sets are designed to do several things the same as slot motions:

1. Force one-on-one situations.
2. Confuse cover assignments.
3. Flood zone areas.
4. Change formation strengths and defensive assignments.

Smooth, simple adjustments to any shifts or motions by the offense must be made by the secondary with confidence. As long as the shifts and motions do not upset or confuse the defense, the offense gains no advantage.

These adjustments are not difficult for our defense and they take away any advantage the offense may gain by changing sets. Adjustments are a necessity for a good secondary.

11

GOAL LINE

The goal line is the most intense battleground on any football field. The greatest boost and momentum changer in football is a *goal line stand*. In order for a defense to make a goal line stand, they must read and execute the defense perfectly and quickly. The defense must swarm to the ball, hit hard and high. They must hit high to keep the ball from falling forward.

The secondary must be ready to destroy any attempt by the offense to penetrate the line of scrimmage. They must also jump on any patterns run by the receivers. Special techniques are used on the goal line to seal receivers off from the quarterback.

We run six goal line alignments. They are used for different goal line situations. Most alignment changes involve the down linemen and the free safety. These alignment changes are necessary to have enough flexibility to handle all of the possible things the offense can do to you. It is almost impossible to have a good goal line defense today if you do only one thing. Flexibility and combinations are required to ensure a strong, determined secondary.

Our first goal line is our sixty goal line. The six refers to the number of down linemen in the defense. The second number (in this case, zero) tells the linemen where to line up.

In all our goal line defenses, our corners, who are covering a wide receiver, are all taught to play the same techniques. We always align our corners one yard inside the receiver and one yard off the ball. From here they play the receiver only. They will not allow the receiver to release to the inside. It is very important that the cornerback does not step toward the receiver as he leaves the line of scrimmage. To step toward him will open the gate for him to escape either inside or outside. The corner must wait for the receiver to come to him to make his contact. If the receiver releases wide to the outside, don't worry about making contact—just run with him and read his face. The corner must lock him outside and stay between him and the quarterback. He must read eyes and hands when the receiver takes him to the outside. If the receiver breaks on a quick out at the goal line, the corner must jump on his heels and force any pass to the receiver to be thrown over the corner's head to the outside. This is the toughest pass on the goal line to complete when the corner can get between the quarterback and receiver. If the receiver tries to release inside, the corner waits until the receiver starts to cross his face; then, he makes contact and drives the receiver inside down the line of scrimmage (Diagram 11:1). If an option shows to the outside and the corner is needed to help, the safety to that side calls RUN! On a run call the corner will release the wide receiver and come back to help on the outside.

The strong safety aligns head up on the tight end. His first read is the tight end. If the tight end blocks down, the strong end will close off the off-tackle hole behind the strong end. The strong safety must move to the outside hip of the strong end. From this position he can help inside or out (Diagram 11:1).

If the tight end tries to release, the strong safety will step up and make contact with him. As he makes contact, the strong safety must look into the backfield for a back out. If a back does show coming on the outside, the strong safety must hold up the tight end until the back crosses his face. When the back crosses his face, the strong safety will

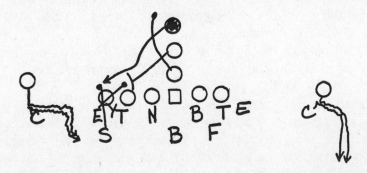

Diagram 11:1. Strong safety moves to a position where he can help inside or out when tight end blocks down.

release the tight end and move to cover the back out. The safety must hold up the tight end to allow time for the middlebacker to get over to cover the tight end. (Diagram 11:2 shows this situation.)

If the tight end tries to release and no back comes to the strong safety's side, the strong safety can stay with the tight end. If the tight end releases and tries to go to the outside, the strong safety must go with him and the middlebacker must now find the back out (Diagram 11:3).

If the tight end blocks out on the strong end, the strong safety must step up behind the end and read to help inside or out. The middlebacker should help close off the off-tackle hole. The strong safety can only help inside when he is sure the ball is coming inside. His responsibility is always outside.

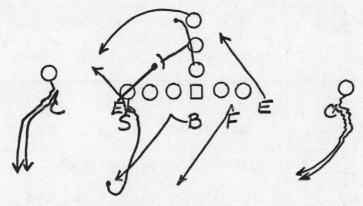

Diagram 11:2. Safety makes and holds contact until the running back crosses his face to the outside.

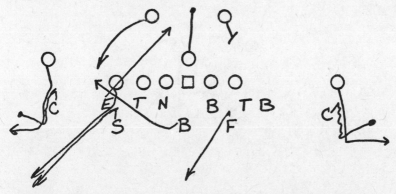

Diagram 11:3. Corner gets between the quarterback and the receivers.

If the flow goes weak and the tight end comes across the middle, the strong safety must go with him. If the flow goes weak and the tight end stays in to block, the strong safety will go to zone in the middle.

The free safety aligns on the inside hip of the defensive tackle and his assignment is second back out. The dive back will be handled by the middlebacker. The quarterback will be taken by the outside backer. Diagram 11:4 shows how our sixty defense handles the weak side veer. As you know the weak side veer is very tough for a true sixty-five goal line to stop.

Diagram 11:5 shows motion and a back out to the weak side.

The goal line requires some special techniques of the secondary as a whole and especially the corners as individuals. Goal line defenses usually involve the safeties in combinations with inside backers or with the weak side end. An example of one such combination is shown in Diagrams 11:2 and 11:3 between the strong safety and inside backer. The corners must be drilled on playing inside position (Chapter 12, Diagram 12:28).

They must also be drilled on playing in front of the receivers on the goal line. Playing behind the receiver on the goal line can only result in a score (Chapter 12, Diagram 12:26).

Receiver combinations from a slot set must be prepared for. We use a technique called *inside-out*. This is shown in Chapter 12, Diagram 12:29.

Another important goal line technique is to teach all secondary personnel and especially safeties to tackle high and knock the ball carrier backwards. Drills for teaching this technique are found in Chapter 12, Diagrams 12:18 and 12:30.

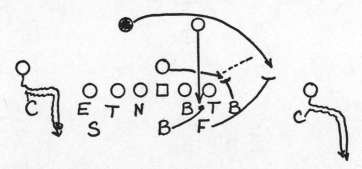

Diagram 11:4. The free safety has the second back out on pass. The outside backer has the first back out.

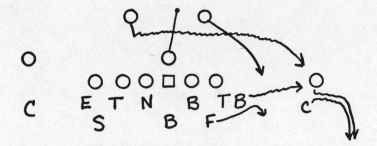

Diagram 11:5. Motion man would be first back out; swingback would be second back out; middlebacker would go to zone.

In our 62-goal line we move our weak backer and noseman into the guard center gaps. The strong backer plays head up on the strong side guard. All other positions on the field are the same (Diagram 11:6).

In the 62, the free safety must plug any dive that shows. This defense is used against a team that likes to run a lot of power offense down the goal line. The free safety fill is shown in Diagram 11:7.

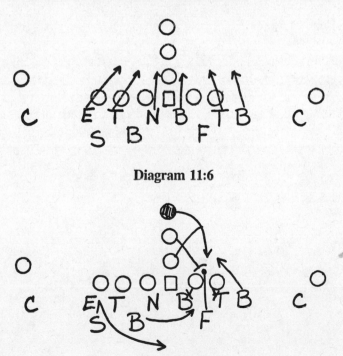

Diagram 11:6

Diagram 11:7

The free safety must be drilled in practice to step up and create a pile in the hole. If you don't work on this practice, you can't expect an athlete who backs up his first two steps on every other play to step up in the hole like a linebacker in this defense. For this reason we sometimes go to double-nose and have the weak backer play the free safety spot.

The 63-goal line requires us to run against a formation with a split end. Diagram 11:8 shows that in the 63-goal line, we gap off the weak side and play our free safety outside our outside backer.

When the free safety lines up outside the outside backer, he now has the first back out to his side. The outside backer now has the second back out. Weak side option is shown in Diagram 11:9. The tackle must be able to stop the dive. Speed option to the weak side is very tough to stop (Diagram 11:10). In Diagram 11:11 we show strong side option coverage out of our 63-defense.

The 64-goal line is used for our goal line slant call. The linebackers are schooled in formation tendencies on the goal line. We call 64-goal line slant. The linebackers must look at the formation when the offense

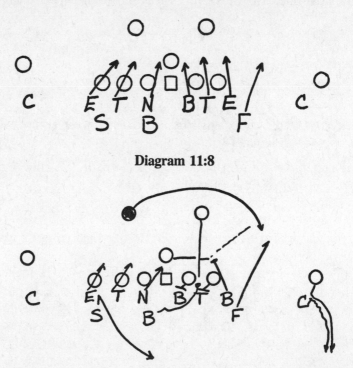

Diagram 11:8

Diagram 11:9. Weak side veer. Backer must look to help on dive.

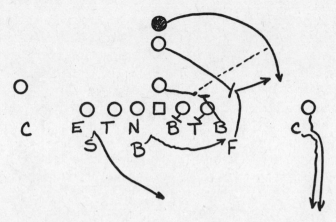

Diagram 11:10. Free safety must be able to play off the lead back's block to make the play.

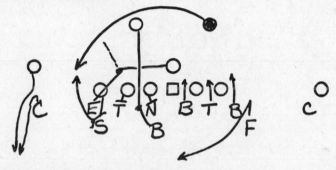

Diagram 11:11. Strong safety must take on the tight end always with his outside shoulder to clear himself to the outside.

comes to the line of scrimmage and make a slant call. We only slant the four down linemen (Diagram 11:12).

We play our middlebacker head up on the center. He must plug the first back into the line on either side. The free safety has outside coverage and first back out. The strong safety's and corner's responsibilities do not change.

Our last alignment is used mostly when a team is inside our two-yard line. It's our sixty-six goal line. The sixty-six is our guts defense. It's our eight-gap. Diagram 11:13 shows the sixty-six against a six-man front. Diagram 11:14 shows the sixty-six against a seven-man front. The free safety has first back out to his side. The strong safety and middle linebacker have their combo cover on the tight end and first back. The tight end must be jammed-up.

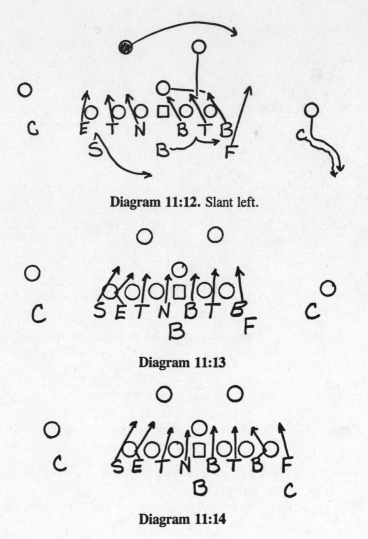

Diagram 11:12. Slant left.

Diagram 11:13

Diagram 11:14

The strong safety moves up on the outside to play as a defensive end. The strong end must step to meet the tight end. The middlebacker must plug any back into the line. He must hit him high to knock him back.

The seven-man front forces our free safety to play the end position. It is most important for the strong safety and free safety to jam the tight ends as they read the play. In order to handle slot sets and two close wide receivers on the goal line, it is necessary to protect our defense from crossing patterns and pick plays.

Our inside-out call originated out of our need to handle these goal line pass situations. In order to have the ability to play a good man-to-man on the goal line and use a counter move for the pick pass, we decided on an eight-yard rule. If two receivers are within eight yards of each other, the safety will call *"inside."* This means that he will take the first receiver to come inside. The corner will take the first receiver to go outside.

The safety must read the combination of both receivers. The corner must play the deepest pattern first until the receivers are committed. Diagram 11:15 shows several possible patterns out of a slot set on the goal line.

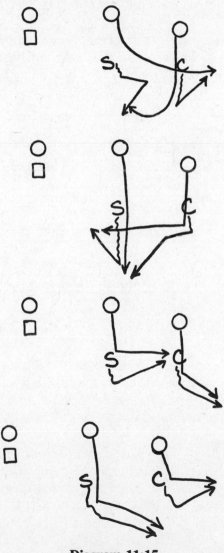

Diagram 11:15

The reactions of the safety and corner must be made quickly to get between the receiver and the quarterback. Goal line pass coverage comes down to wanting to prevent a score and doing everything in your power to prevent your man from scoring.

When many teams get into a goal line situation it is very evident they don't believe they can stop anyone. I played on a defensive team in 1968 that made 13 goal line stands. We believed no one could score on us. *We believed in our coaches and in each other*. Thirteen times we turned teams away. We knew that when everyone did his job we couldn't be scored upon. How did we know? Our coaches believed it and they told us so!

The *key* to teaching pass coverage anywhere on the field comes down to the coach's knowing and believing in what he is teaching.

12

DRILLS

Drills are the backbone of any football position. However, the defensive backfield coach must use them daily to improve speed, flexibility, and especially, the footwork of the backs he coaches.

Many coaches use drills that are, in my opinion, a waste of time. A drill such as the tip drill takes up time that could be used on more important ones. I feel that if I have to drill my defensive backs to go after, or react to, a tipped ball, then I have the wrong athletes on the field. You can't drill just to fill in time. You must drill to improve on individual weaknesses.

The following are drills which we have used to improve and prepare our defensive backs for general and specific game situations.

Everyday Drills for Agility

1. *Back Pedal*—The proper back pedal must be worked on everyday: Bent knees, bent at the waist with the body weight over the knees. Body weight must be forward. The weight must be forward to allow the defensive back to drive forward on any move by a receiver in front of him. If a defensive back is allowed to retreat with his weight back on his heels, it will take him at least two steps to throw his weight forward so he can attack. The defensive back must be taught to drive his arms as he back pedals. This improves his speed and balance.

2. *Quick Feet Drill*—This drill is designed to work the defensive back's feet. In this drill the back tries to keep his shoulders square as he backs straight back. The defensive back will rotate his hips as he crosses

and uncrosses his feet during his retreat. The lead foot goes behind as the hips rotate from side to side. His next step is across in front of his first step. His third step is to open and square his feet. The fourth step is straight back. His fifth step is to cross in front of his fourth step as his hips cross to the other side. His sixth step is open and his seventh step is back again. The eighth step is across in front (Diagram 12:1).

3. *Mashed Potatoes*—This drill is the same foot movement as the Quick Feet Drill. The only difference is that in Mashed Potatoes the athlete must move his feet as quickly as possible. The footsteps are the same as in Diagram 12:1.

4. *Drive Drill*—In this drill you have four lines that on the snap of the ball back pedal until the coach turns his shoulders. At that point, the defensive backs break forward on a 45-degree angle. The most important coaching point is a *short jab step* for breaking the backward movement and pushing off to start the forward attack (Diagram 12:2). Most coaches work on backward movements to the deep, but few work on the important forward movements. The jab step must be taught. It is a quick break and drive. As long as the body weight is kept over the hips, the forward shift can be made easily. It is important to teach the short jab because a long step takes too much time and there is a good chance the defensive back will slip and fall. The jab step will make the difference between interception and completion.

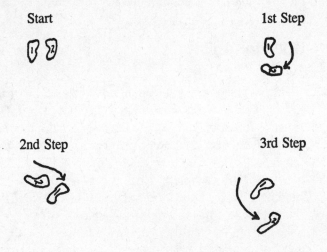

Diagram 12:1

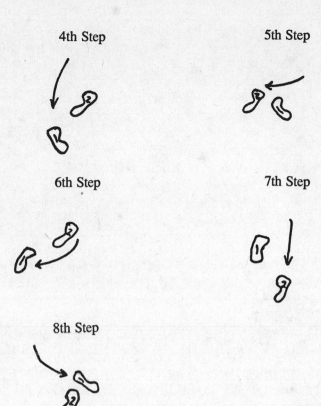

4th Step

5th Step

6th Step

7th Step

8th Step

Diagram 12:1 (continued)

Diagram 12:2

5. *Turn to the Deep*—Touchdown passes in many cases could be prevented if the defensive back knew the proper technique for turning with the receiver to run deep. This is most important. We run this drill every day. The defensive back must try to maintain his back pedal as long as possible. Once the receiver gets within three yards of the defensive back, the defensive back must turn with him and run stride for stride with him. Always looking into his face, the defensive back must watch the receiver not the quarterback, once the receiver has committed to the deep route (Diagrams 12:3 and 12:4).

The defensive back must keep his eyes on the receiver at all times. To check for this we have the receivers run the Z out and the squirrel pattern. If the defensive back takes his eyes off the receiver, he will lose him.

    a. This drill can be and should be run with the turn to the deep drill. We call this our *Read-the-Face Drill*. In this drill we

Diagram 12:3

Diagram 12:4

ST
TYKIE

DONNIE

ROBT

LUTHER
TREY

WK
AERION

MIKE

have the receiver run a deep route. The defensive back must turn and run stride for stride with the receiver, looking at his face. The defensive back does not look for the ball until the receiver does. The defensive back must make slight contact with his hips against the receiver as he turns to look for the ball. This is done by leaning backward into the receiver when the defensive turns his head to look for the ball. The contact is to lock the receiver off. This keeps the defensive back between the receiver and the ball, and also allows the defensive back to feel the receiver if he tries to fade to the outside when the defensive back turns to look back at the quarterback.

6. *Playing the Hands*—This drill can be incorporated with the turn-to-the-deep and read-the-receiver's face drills. In this drill we put the defensive back in a position where he is beaten by two yards. In this situation we teach him not to look for the ball when the receiver looks. If the defensive back looks and the ball is thrown on target, he has no play. If the ball is thrown short, he may miss an interception but his body will prevent a completion. The main reason for not looking for the ball is that we want the defensive back to play the hands of the receiver. When beaten, the defensive back can gain ground on the receiver when he looks for the ball. The reason he can gain ground when the receiver looks is because he crosses his hips in order to look back at the quarterback. This will slow him down. By not looking, the defensive back will not cross his hips and he can close on the receiver. We teach the defensive back, when beaten, to play the hands of the receiver. That is, to watch for the receiver to form a basket to catch the ball. This will tell the defensive back if the ball is high or low. Once the defensive back sees the basket, he must get a hand into the basket and pull a hand of the receiver away. This will break up the catch. The timing between the moment when the defensive back sees the basket and makes a play for the receiver's hands is very close to the time the ball arrives. When used properly, this technique can save many big plays or touchdowns.

7. *Playing the Pattern*—Here we use many patterns: sideline; up; slant; post; flag; curl; etc. We work the hardest on the patterns the team we are going to play favors. We always teach playing the upfield shoulder on any pattern. The upfield shoulder is the shoulder closest to the goal line in the direction the receiver is going. We want our defensive

backs to first identify the pattern and quickly work themselves to the receiver's upfield shoulder. From here the defensive back can play both the receiver and the ball (Diagram 12:5).

If the receiver runs an out and up, and the defensive back drives on the out move, he is in perfect position to break up the deep move by the receiver, if he is driving on the upfield shoulder (Diagram 12:6).

The defensive back will only knock the receiver off his route if he feels he has overcommitted to the out move and cannot turn to run with the receiver's deep move. Pattern drills are important to teach the proper footwork necessary to attack each pattern.

8. *Pattern Combinations*—It is most important that common pattern combinations and your opponent's favorite combinations are taught. When you're using zone covers, you must teach combinations to prevent your defensive backs from guarding unoccupied zones. By teaching combinations and reading receivers, the defensive backs can read the intended pattern early and begin to cheat to the primary receiv-

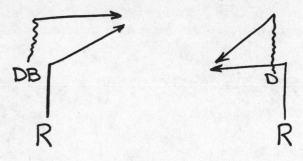

Diagram 12:5

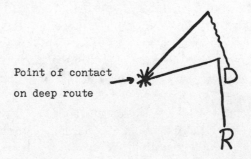

Diagram 12:6. Point of contact on deep route.

ing zones. A common pattern run from slot sets is shown in Diagram 12:7. Diagram 12:8 shows how a normal invert cover would cover the pattern. Diagram 12:9 shows how a reading secondary can react to pattern combinations.

Strong safety reads the up pattern from the slot back and realizes the combination calls for a curl from the wide receiver. He checks outside first, and then breaks to the curl. There are many pattern combinations that can be taught. However, there are five that must be taught to the cornerbacks if you are going to run a zone defense. We call these patterns *sucker patterns*. Diagram 12:10 shows the basic five sucker patterns:

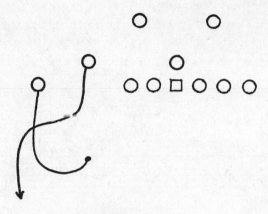

Diagram 12:7

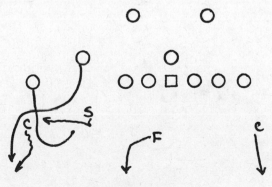

Diagram 12:8

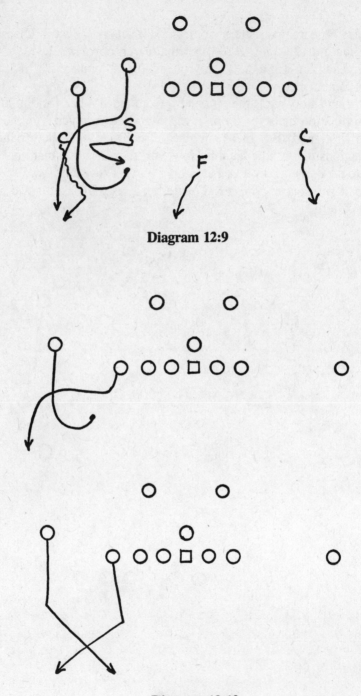

Diagram 12:9

Diagram 12:10

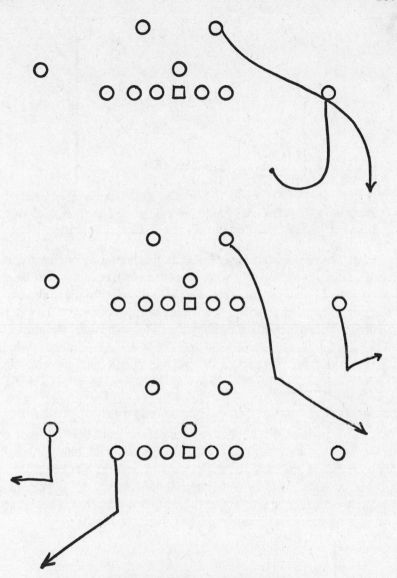

Diagram 12:10 (continued)

The attempt by the offense in these patterns is to draw the corner-backs out of position with one receiver and then slip another receiver by them. They must be schooled to read, not just cover a deep area.

9. *Sweep Drill*—This drill is designed to prepare the cornerbacks and the strong safety to attack blockers and keep their feet in order to make the tackle (Diagram 12:11).

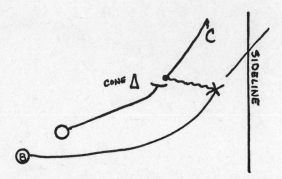

Diagram 12:11. The corner must meet the blocker head-on, but move to protect the outside. Zone to sideline is about 12 yards.

10. *Step-by Technique*—It seems that many of our best corner-backs are small athletes. We don't want our small corners meeting large fullbacks head-on all night. We came up with a technique to protect our little cornerbacks and still allow them to do their jobs. The step-by technique demands a quick read by the defensive back. He must close quickly on the line of scrimmage and break down. He must set up in a hitting position before the back can get into position to throw his block. The split second before the blocking back makes contact with the cornerback, the corner steps by him. Most backs are moving much too fast to adjust to this movement (Diagram 12:12).

11. This is a drill that teaches our defensive backs that when they are the last man, they can't attack the blocker and hold their ground. The defensive back must back pedal, control and slow the blocker to slow the ball-carrier down. In this manner help should arrive. It is important that the defensive backs be taught that there are times when it is necessary to give ground to make the *sure tackle* (Diagram 12:13).

Diagram 12:12. It's important that the DB gives the blocking back a good set target before he steps by.

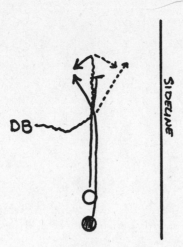

Diagram 12:13

12. *Reaction to the Ball*—In this drill the defensive back retreats on the snap straight back past two placed receivers. When the coach turns his shoulders to one of the receivers, the defensive back plants and drives to intercept the pass (Diagram 12:14).

13. *Flag Drill*—This drill helps increase the distance the defensive back can travel while the ball is in the air. On the snap, the defensive back starts to back pedal until the coach turns his shoulders from side-to-side. As the coach does so, the defensive back opens on a 45-degree angle to the side to which the coach is looking (Diagram 12:15).

14. *Stretching the Deep Cover*—This drill is used to teach the defensive backs to cover the middle of their deep zone until the quarterback commits to a receiver. It also helps develop the defensive back's ability to cover ground while the ball is in the air (Diagram 12:16).

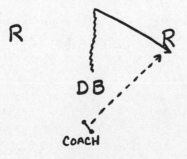

Diagram 12:14

Diagram 12:15. When the ball is thrown the DB must fly to the ball while it's in air. This drill can be run with four DBs at a time.

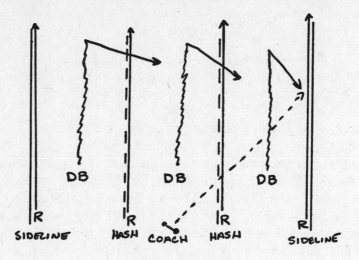

Diagram 12:16

15. *Reading the Passer's Eyes*—In this drill the defensive backs are placed in the middle of a semicircle. The coach will make eye contact with one of the players in the semicircle, just before throwing him the ball. The defensive back must read the eyes and get to the receiver (Diagram 12:17).

16. *Form Tackling*—To teach the proper techniques in tackling is of prime importance. These techniques must be taught, not to make better tacklers, but to make safer tacklers. Tackling is an art. It must be taught in the proper steps to insure the safety of the athlete. The knees

should be bent, the hips must be lower than those of the ball carrier. The back must be straight with the head up and the neck bowed. The athlete must explode into the tackle.

17. *Peek-a-Boo Drill*—This drill is used to teach the seeking out of the ball carrier and stepping up to make the hit with the proper form (Diagram 12:18).

18. *Mirror Drill*—This drill is to teach proper position on the receiver's upfield shoulder as the receiver changes direction. The defensive back must work to get to the upfield shoulder (Diagram 12:19).

19. *Rotate to Deep* (mirror the quarterback)—This drill is a good zone drill. It is very good for teaching a safety to mirror the quarterback and stay deep over the ball (Diagram 12:20).

20. *Throw Back Drill*—We use this drill to train our corners on proper position when flow goes away from them. We teach our corners

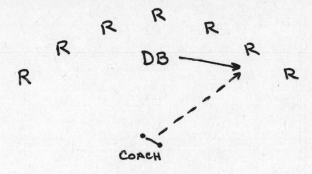

Diagram 12:17

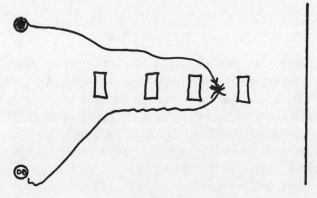

Diagram 12:18

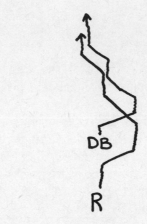

Diagram 12:19

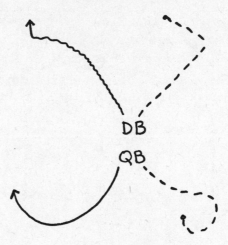

Diagram 12:20

to give a seven- to ten-yard cushion when both backs go away. If the receiver breaks to the post, the defensive back will drive on his upfield shoulder. If the receiver tries to run deep, the cornerback keeps his cushion and plays the ball when it goes up (Diagram 12:21).

21. *Two-on-One*—This is a drill to teach the safety to stay at home and play the deepest route. In this drill one receiver always runs deep. You can rush both deep from time-to-time (Diagram 12:22). In this drill we give one receiver the option of three different routes.

We add to this drill by putting a linebacker in it to read the quarterback and find the under route (Diagram 12:23).

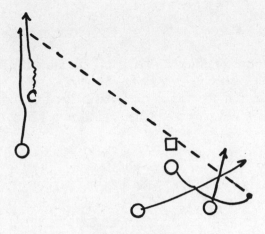

Diagram 12:21

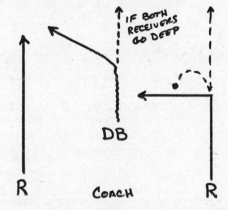

IF BOTH RECEIVERS GO DEEP

DB

R   COACH   R

Diagram 12:22

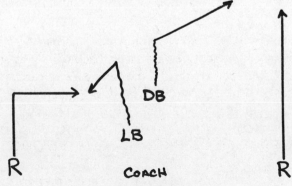

DB

LB

R   COACH   R

Diagram 12:23

22. *Shoulder-to-Shoulder*—This drill works on man cover for the post and flag patterns. In this drill the defensive back starts even, looking into the receiver's face. The defensive back is totally dependent on reading the receiver to find the ball (Diagram 12:24).

23. *Quarterback Release Read*—We work on teaching the quarterback release from the line of scrimmage. Reading the release gives quick clues as to the play possibilities (Diagram 12:25).

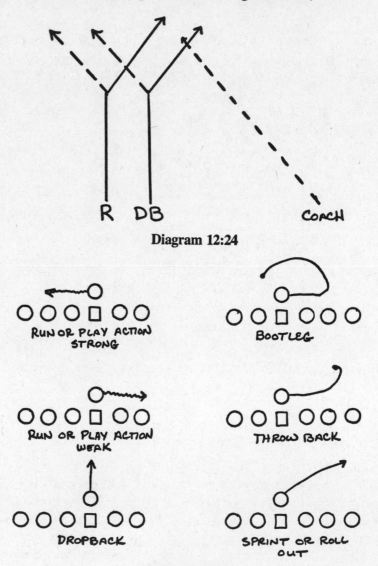

Diagram 12:24

RUN OR PLAY ACTION STRONG

BOOTLEG

RUN OR PLAY ACTION WEAK

THROW BACK

DROPBACK

SPRINT OR ROLL OUT

Diagram 12:25

24. *Tight End Read Drill*—A drill that is useful and must be run to school the strong safety on his reads is our tight end drill. In this drill the tight end has five moves:

    a. Block Down.
    b. Hook Block.
    c. Turnout Block.
    d. Inside Release.
    e. Outside Release.

The strong safety and our weak corner (against a slot) have the same reads. Each move by the tight end tells the strong safety or weak corner what he is to do (Diagram 12:26).

Situation A Block Down

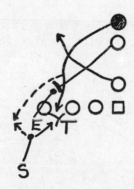

Diagram 12:26. Safety should be able to play both inside and outside run.

Situation B Blocking Back Hooks

The strong safety must step up to one yard off his end, close and read near back. If the back tries to kick-out block, the strong safety looks for the ball inside. He cannot commit to the inside until he reads the ball inside. He still has outside responsibility. If the lead blocker (guard or fullback) tries to hook the end, the safety moves outside (Diagram 12:27).

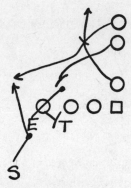

Diagram 12:27

Situation C Hook Block

If the tight end tries to hook, the strong safety must attack straight ahead as soon as his read is made. He must beat the block of the wide receiver (Diagram 12:28).

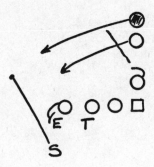

Diagram 12:28. Safety comes right now on hook block. He must beat the block-down of the wide receiver.

Situation D Turnout Block

If the tight end tries to turn our defensive end out, our strong safety must step up and read the back's move (Diagram 12:29).

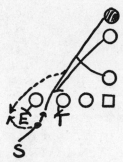

Diagram 12:29. If back appears in the hole, the strong safety must tackle him. If the back bounces outside, the strong safety must make that play also.

Situation E Inside Release

If the tight end takes an inside release, the strong safety must retreat and look into the backfield. If a man cover is called, he must go with the tight end. If a reading zone is called and both backs have gone away from him, he must retreat to deep middle (Diagram 12:30).

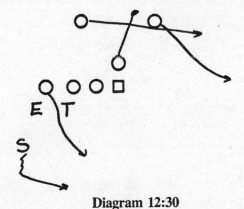

Diagram 12:30

Situation F Outside Release

If an outside release is read, the strong safety must attack the tight end first and then read for run or pass. If outside release is for a run, it's probably going to be an option and the tight end is going to block the safety. By attacking him, we take away his block. If the tight end takes an outside release and it's for a pass, it's most likely a tight end seam from play action. By attacking him, we give our linebackers time to get out and we destroy the timing of the pass (Diagram 12:31).

We use these same reads for our weak corners in a slot set (Diagram 12:32).

These are drills that we use every week. At any time we feel that our secondary is lacking in any area of play, we will design a drill to improve that area of our game. We have many group drills and half-time drills that we run with our linebackers and ends. These are designed to coordinate our covers. Basic to all outstanding secondaries are outstanding athletes and coaching that takes nothing for granted, and drills for every situation.

25. *Chase Drill*—In this drill we teach a defensive player who is beaten not to give up, but to play the receiver for his move to the ball (Diagram 12:33).

The defensive player must step in front of the receiver when he makes his move. By doing this the defensive player has a good chance to

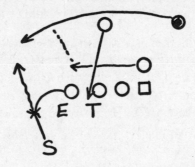

Diagram 12:31. The strong safety must hit the tight end square.

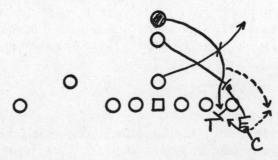

Diagram 12:32. Same reads in this set for weak corner.

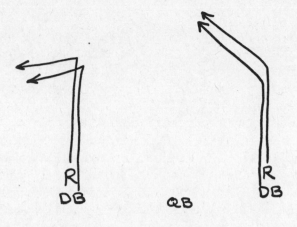

Diagram 12:33

knock the ball down if it is not thrown perfectly. He must work to stay between the receiver and quarterback when he is beaten. This can cause an overthrow, knocked-down pass or at least impair the receiver's vision of the ball. Any of these can save a big play.

26. *Corner Short Zone*—This drill is designed to teach the corner-backs to play the short zones in Covers 6, 7, 8 and 9. The corner must first make contact with the wide receiver as he releases from the line of scrimmage. The minute the corner makes contact he must get his head up and look for the near back. If the near back is coming out into a pattern, the corner can't drop as deep. If the back is staying in, the corner can drop to about 12 yards deep. He is still responsible for a screen to his side. A soon as the corner has checked for the back out, he now must read the quarterback and move inside or out in the short zone (Diagram 12:34). This technique is the same for the short zone corner in Covers 6, 7, 8 and 9.

Corner must play between receivers. He plays off the back and in front of the wide receiver, reading the quarterback. If the quarterback opens his shoulders to the back and takes his lead hand off the ball, the corner must drive on the back. If the quarterback doesn't open to the back the corner must keep working to the outside with the deeper receiver.

27. *Goal Line Inside Technique*—The corner positions line up one yard off the receiver and on his inside shoulder. The corner never steps forward or strikes at the receiver's release. To step forward and miss would be a disaster. The corner takes two quick steps in retreat. This

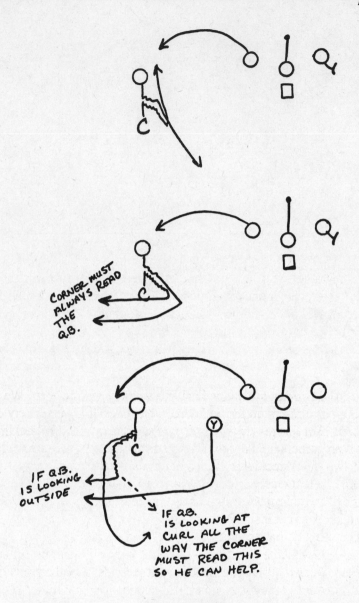

Diagram 12:34

allows for any quick fakes by the receiver on his release. If the receiver crosses the corner's face, the corner must make contact and drive the receiver back into the line of scrimmage. If the receiver releases outside, the corner must get between the receiver and the quarterback. The corner then reads the receiver's face and plays his hands (Diagram 12:35).

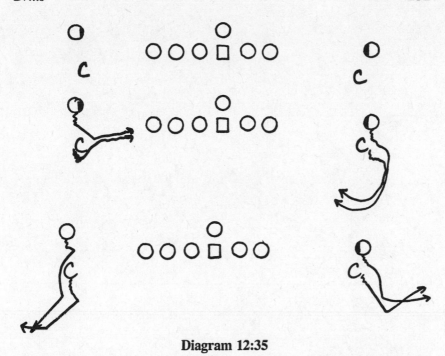

Diagram 12:35

28. *Inside-out*—On the goal line we play man-to-man. We prefer to play our corners on the wide receivers and our strong safety on the tight end. For this reason when we play against a slot on the goal line, we play both corners on the slot and our strong safety on the tight end side. With two quick receivers in close alignment, the possibility of a pick pattern or a lost receiver in a crossing pattern is a very real problem. We handle this problem with our inside-out call. Inside-out means the inside man takes the first inside pattern man-to-man and the outside man takes the first outside pattern man-to-man (Diagram 12:36).

30. *Goal Line Tackling*—The goal line is the hardest hit area on the field. Decisions must be made in split seconds. A ball carrier allowed to fall forward could mean a play that was stopped at the line of scrimmage is now a touchdown. For this reason secondary personnel must be drilled on goal line tackling. It's not enough just to tackle on the goal line. The running backs must be knocked backward, or at least sideways. For this drill, pile four large dummies up two yards from the goal line. Don't allow the ball carriers to line up more than two yards from the bags. The defenders should be no more than two yards from the bags. If they get too far apart, you'll get tremendous hits but you may not have any backs left. Remember, the objective of drills is to teach and prepare,

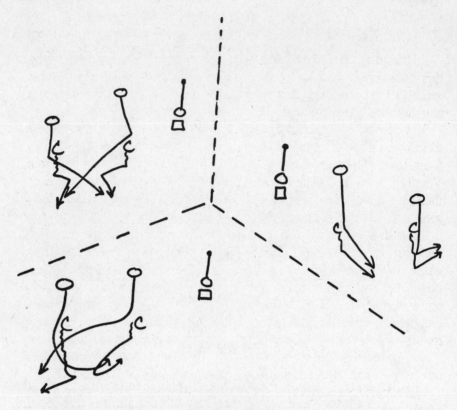

Diagram 12:36

not destroy. The ball carrier runs either straight at the high point of the bags and dives into the end zone or runs on an angle right off the outside of the bags. The defensive back must meet the ball over the bags and turn him back. If the back is slanting into the end zone outside the bags, the defensive back must take the proper angle and knock the back laterally (Diagram 12:37).

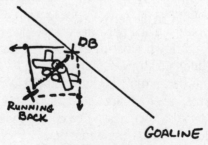

Diagram 12:37

SUMMARY

In summation, if the techniques, principles and covers discussed in this book are taught in the proper sequence, they will provide your secondary with enough flexibility to adjust easily to any formation or situation and a high potential for success can be anticipated.

I do not, however, suggest you should try to implement all these techniques and covers in just one season. Work with Cover 1 and Cover 4 on Lower Division teams as well as the Varsity. Teach your Junior Varsity Covers 1, 2, 3 and 7 along with Cover 4. The following season, then, it should be easier to add Covers 8 and 9, saving Cover 6 for a special change of pace cover vs. a good slot team.

With some hard work, multiple offensive sets can be met with multiple defensive covers. The multiple covers prevent the offense from easily running receivers into predetermined open areas. With the offense now forced to read the defense or add special patterns to beat a specific cover we may or may not be in, the possibilities for an offensive mistake are greatly increased. Due to the complexities involved in trying to beat multiple covers, chances for the defense's success are greatly improved.

The multiple cover system gives you a choice of covers on a crucial down. You can blitz and hurry the passer or drop off and cover.

Formation recognition and a simple system for adjusting to the many varied forms of motion are of primary importance if you are to have a solid, aggressive secondary.

Special care must be taken to explain, instruct and correct goal line covers. Covers which are good in midfield do not provide the necessary time and distance relative to the goal line to be effective.

When all is said and done, it is the coach and his attention to details that make for a great secondary. You must believe in what you decide to teach, have faith in your athletes and accept nothing less than the best effort possible from them. All this must be accomplished with a positive attitude. You can't play in the secondary without skills, aggressiveness, desire and above all confidence.

INDEX

185